ESCAPING THE PRICE-DRIVEN SALE

ESCAPING THE PRICE-DRIVEN SALE

How World-Class Sellers Create Extraordinary Profit

By Tom Snyder and Kevin Kearns

New York   Chicago   San Francisco
Lisbon   London   Madrid   Mexico City   Milan
New Delhi   San Juan   Seoul   Singapore
Sydney   Toronto

1 2 3 4 5 6 7 8 9 0   DOC/DOC   0 9 8 7

ISBN-13: 978-0-07-154583-9
MHID: 0-07-154583-2

McGraw-Hill books are available at special quantity discounts to use as premiums and sales promotions, or for use in corporate training programs. For more information, please write to the Director of Special Sales, Professional Publishing, McGraw-Hill, Two Penn Plaza, New York, NY 10121-2298. Or contact your local bookstore.

This book is printed on acid-free paper.

Contents

ESCAPING THE PRICE-DRIVEN SALE

PART 1

VALUE CREATION AND THE CONSULTATIVE SELLER

CHAPTER 1

WHAT THE CUSTOMER WANTS

Full fathom five thy father lies:

Of his bones are coral made:

Those are pearls that were his eyes:

Nothing of him that doth fade

But doth suffer a sea-change

Into something rich and strange.

—SHAKESPEARE, *The Tempest*

Current statistics indicate that there are approximately 417 sales professionals for every senior executive in the United States. The vast majority of these sellers will compete on price alone. This book will discuss what research has revealed about the very few among those 417 sales professionals who actually do escape the price-driven sale.

ADMIRAL HIRAM G. RICKOVER, the father of the nuclear Navy, was an eccentric genius. His interview tactics for screening candidates for the elite nuclear submarine program were as excruciating as they were unorthodox. Indeed, he is famous for saying, "The more you sweat in peace, the less you sweat in war," and he ruthlessly applied the principle in his infamous stress interview process. There was method to the legendary madness: he wanted to evaluate his people under conditions of extreme stress—only those with superior qualifications could be considered. Occasionally he would leap out of a closet to surprise an unsuspecting candidate. Sometimes he would nail a chair to the floor, and when the applicant arrived in his darkened office, he would greet him with "Pull up a chair, Captain." Or he would saw one or two inches off the front legs of the interviewee's chair and watch him squirm as he slid forward while trying to maintain composure in the face of a withering barrage of questions. He was not above banishing a candidate to the broom closet to think over an inelegant answer.

He would often begin an interview by asking the nervous candidate what subject he knew most about in the world. It could be any subject at all, from gardening lettuce to the structure of the cosmos. "Take care with your answer," he would say. "For whatever you choose, I shall know more about it than you!" And he would. For Admiral Rickover was a particularly brilliant man, who studied the profiles of his prospective crew members and made it his business to read more about their particular areas of expertise than they had likely read themselves. The interviews would sometimes last for three days.

Customers are now able to sit in judgment like the great admiral. If they so desire, they can truthfully say to the hapless salesperson, "I know more about your product or service than you do! What else do you have to offer that I should bother wasting my time with you?" So customers have two choices: either they don't see a salesperson, and buy everything that they want to buy transactionally, or else they gain something from the sales experience itself. Ideally, they will gain insight, analysis, and expertise that they cannot get anywhere else. It is the value of the expertise that they want: it is not the easily accessible product or service expertise that they are looking for; it is *sales* expertise. That is what customers care about.

What is it then that makes the sales experience worthwhile? What are the things that a salesperson has in her possession that can't be gotten by any other means than by interacting and that the customer can't reach in any other way than by that interaction? It is what the salesperson understands about the marketplace; it is what she understands about a customer's peculiar competition; it is what she understands about the business that the customer cannot acquire through any other means.

How could customers possibly understand the competitive landscape that they face in the same way that a good salesperson does? They can't. Because the salesperson is looking, day after day, at the world in which the customers compete, she has a perspective that just can't be duplicated either by an Internet search or even by some sort of pure consultancy. It is unique, and if rendered properly, it can ensure a long-term, profitable relationship.

THE AVAILABILITY OF INFORMATION

At the end of the day the customer ultimately wants one of two things: (1) the cheapest price or (2) the best value. It's that simple *and* that complex. With the advent of the Internet, customer attitudes toward buying (and toward salespeople) have changed drastically. In many cases, salespeople have become obsolete. The following is a simple illustration.

Consider for a moment that you are in the market for a new banker. Google "corporate banking." In 0.28 seconds, it returns 1,190,000 results. Today's consumers can find out everything they want to know, and indeed, everything there is to know, about "corporate banking" from products and services to the best prices on the planet. Literally. In seconds. At their fingertips. In fact, reading an average of one page every 40 seconds, it would take 1.5 years without rest to read just the first page of every result for "corporate banking".

Then try these:

- "Data processing": 28,600,000 results in 0.27 seconds

- "Accounting": 198,000,000 in 0.29 seconds

- "Management consulting": 2,150,000 in 0.27 seconds

- "Packaging": 110,000,000 in 0.27 seconds

- "Health care": 102,000,000 in 0.33 seconds

It's hard to know how much useful information is contained in all those hits, but it seems pretty certain that it's far beyond the capacity of any individual to absorb. And thanks to the algorithms used by Google, most of the vital information is fairly likely to be contained in the first few pages of results. Search engines today are so sophisticated that they can ferret out exactly what we're looking for in fractions of a second. A buyer can put together a very clear picture of options in any industry imaginable in a very short period of time.

Thus, if the customers are merely looking for the cheapest price, they really don't ever need to see a salesperson. They can let their fingers do the walking. But suppose they are looking for something more than just the lowest price. Suppose they need more than an academic understanding of their problems, and they are looking for insight, help, and guidance. They are really searching for business alternatives. Suppose they want something more from the buying experience than participation in a reverse auction (many sellers, one buyer). Enter the salesperson of the twenty-first century.

THE CUSTOMER DOESN'T CARE

Most everyone, even first-year economics majors, would accept this simple equation:

Value = Benefits − Cost

Indeed, it has been called "the unassailable value equation." Of course, it is by no means unassailable, as there are probably no two people who agree absolutely on what all three components of the equation actually mean. We shall not get into the argument. And in fact, we will use the equation in a slightly different way than it is normally used. We will use the equation in the context of the buying *experience* rather than in the context of the product or service being sold. So *cost* from this perspective has nothing to do with "price," per se. "Price" is the word usually associated with what you pay for a product or service. From the standpoint of the buying experience itself, there is a different kind of price; here, the cost side of the equation refers to the *time* and *effort* that the customer is devoting to being *sold to*; the energy he is putting into the purchasing *experience*. The *benefits* side of the equation refers to the *insight* and *discovery* that the customer receives from the buying experience.

The challenge for the salesperson in this context is to provide benefits such that they outweigh the investment that the customer is making in the selling experience. In Figure 1.1, the letter *A* represents a sales interaction in which the customer receives a great deal of insight and discovery for what he perceives to be a relatively low cost in time and effort, making it a highly valuable investment. *B* represents a buying experience that is a fair trade-off of cost and benefits. *C* represents a waste of time and effort for the customer because the payoff is not equal to or greater than the cost. It is vital that the sales experience itself produce value to the customer—else why interact with a salesperson at all?

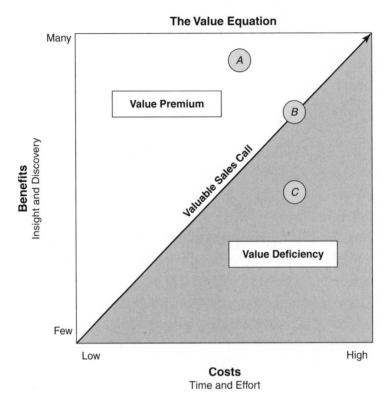

Figure 1.1

If the salesperson doesn't or can't facilitate enough insight and discovery (both of which we shall consider in great detail later) in the selling process to outweigh the customer's investment of time and effort, then the customer will simply seek cheaper and cheaper experiences—the cheapest of which eliminates the salesperson altogether. This equation explains the proliferation of reverse auctions, bidding opportunities, and commodity sales on the Internet: customers are saying, "I get nothing from the selling experience, so I'm not investing in it anymore."

Prior to the Internet phenomenon, any information or knowledge about a product or service was accessible only from a salesperson. Of course, you could glean information from magazine articles and advertisements, or you could spend time researching in the public library. But the former provided incomplete information, and the latter was too expensive in terms of time and effort. So the value that you placed on the salesperson was a kind of Faustian bargain—you *had* to meet with him. If you wanted to understand the opportunities, products, or services available to you, you simply had no other option but to meet with the salesperson. Today you have to meet with no one.

And so we return to the Value Equation: unless the customer is getting from the sales experience itself something that she cannot get in any other way, then she won't participate in it. And why should she? Salespeople are responding by trying to bring more to the table in terms of knowledge—by being better and better at talking about their products or services. *The customer doesn't care*—she's got more data at her fingertips, literally millions of bits of data, than the salesperson could ever possibly know.

THE BAR IS RAISED ON FOREKNOWLEDGE

The customer's world has drastically and irrevocably changed, but the salesperson's world has not kept up. The customer no longer needs the salesperson to give product or service information. And, in fact, customers have very little time or patience for the salesperson that does not approach them fully armed with all the relevant information about the customers' own situation, let alone the salesperson's. The demand for the salesperson's foreknowledge has gone up twentyfold. A salesperson can't walk in and ask simple information-gathering questions anymore. Any relevant question today is asked simply to set the context for the customer's insight. Today, if a salesperson greets a customer with this, "So tell me about *blah blah blah* in your business," the customer's initial reaction is going to be, "There are a hundred ways to find that out!

Why didn't you know that before you came in here? I have no time to waste with you." It is a fact of business life that few salespeople seem to have picked up yet.

Our time is more valuable today than it has ever been before. And that statement is meant in quite a literal sense. We work more and more hours, rush our lunches or eat them at our desks, answer e-mails during conference calls, and generally multitask to the point of insanity. Time is money, and every minute has a dollar value associated with it. Every moment is precious. The salesperson had better have done his homework before he walks into a prospective customer's business.

The bar has been raised substantially. Information-gathering questions that in the past could have been used by salespeople to understand the customer's business better are no longer appropriate. Now such questions must be used only to set the context—to prepare customers to achieve self-discovery. Questions that ask about facts and information available in other places will immediately paint the salesperson who asks them as a commodity and irrelevant; he will be dismissed out of hand. We as customers demand much more for our time. We are busy. As Michael Mandel, chief economist at *BusinessWeek*, says, we are "running as fast as we can to keep pace with a business world turbocharged by technology." Salespeople need to wake up to the new reality. They need to be prepared to know a lot more about their customer's business from the outset than they ever did in the past. The modern customer will not tolerate what will appear as ineptitude.

THE BAR IS ALSO RAISED ON HUMILITY

The new buying community is, as we have seen, increasingly more sophisticated. And extremely knowledgeable. The salesperson must adapt to the new customer or fail. Customers will not tolerate being talked down to because they no longer recognize the salesperson as the expert. When a salesperson comes into a situation and he has the expertise, his tendency is to preach it. And his tendency is to ask questions that sound—to most customers—like rather patronizing questions. "I was reading through your annual report, and I noticed that your margins on sales are lower than any of your competitors. Is that accurate? Let me tell you how I think we can help." Well, my answer to you would be along these lines: "You don't understand this at all; you don't understand the stresses we're under; you don't understand our ownership, our shareholders—there are a million things in here that you simply do not understand!"

The more humble, and professional, question in today's context would be something that sounds more like this: "You know, I've taken some time to go through your financial statements and the publicly available information I could find on both your company and your market sector such as I understand them. I was wondering if I could ask you a couple of questions about some things that I thought were intriguing, especially given the kinds of things that we have seen in similar markets?"

In addition, it is important to know that all kinds of buying decisions have been steadily moving down the food chain from executives to middle and lower management. Executives are increasingly focusing their attention on enterprise-level decisions and on positioning their company in the most competitive posture possible. With that in mind, most executives will not tolerate egotism and pride in salespeople. It is becoming an evermore common occurrence that "C suite" executives are leading enterprise-level relationships.

As far back as 1995, Alston Gardner and Jay Klompmaker from the Kenan-Flagler Business School at the University of North Carolina completed a formidable research study of senior executives and their buying involvement. Gardner and Klompmaker

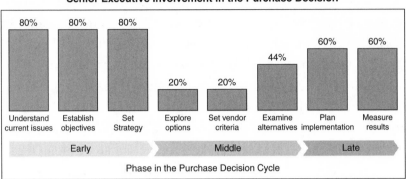

Figure 1.2
Source: Alston Gardner and Jay Klompmaker, "Selling to Senior Executives," research paper, 1995.

subsequently published a research paper entitled "Selling to Senior Executives." Some of their conclusions are depicted in the graph in Figure 1.2.

As you can see in the graph, senior executives are very likely to get involved early in the purchase decision cycle when they are trying to understand current issues, establish objectives, and set strategy. They then get involved again later during the implementation phase and results measurement. Senior executives have more and more of a vested interest in the outcomes of business-to-business selling.

In other words, salespeople seeking to make anything other than purely transactional (that is, priced-based) sales can expect to find themselves negotiating with top-level executives in the modern age. And at the back end, the salespeople had better be able to prove that they have solved a business issue! Good sellers now need to have the capacity to think like and converse in the language of senior executives if they are to escape a purely price-driven sales environment.

The bar has been raised in two dimensions: The first is that you render your insight and expertise because insight and expertise are what both the C suite and the business-to-business buyer crave. And the second is that you render your expertise *humbly*—don't sound like you're preaching or dictating to the customer. In the past, customers suffered from a degree of ignorance regarding products and services. Today, buyers do not suffer from ignorance of products and services but rather from an incomplete understanding of the environment in which they operate. They need your insight, but not coupled with an *I'm-your-savior-thank-God-I-got-here-in-time* sort of attitude. We are beyond that. It no longer serves.

ESCAPING THE PRICE-DRIVEN SALE

Let's tie all of this together by saying that to escape price-driven selling and succeed in the early twenty-first century, sellers need a set of skills that will help them bring extraordinary value into the selling arena and deliver it effectively to their customers.

Huthwaite is a company born of research, and that research effort continues to grow to this day. It is the research of collecting real-world data from real-world people about real-live selling situations (not situations contrived in laboratories). In this book we will describe the conclusions drawn from our years of research into seller and buyer behavior. We have developed insight into a new definition of "customer value" by assembling data on several thousand transactions that had a curious common characteristic. Specifically, we looked at transactions across a wide variety of industries (including those that are product and service driven) that met two criteria:

- The customer reported that in an effort to purchase a particular product, service, or bundle of capabilities, he was faced with a group of competitors seeking his business whose offerings all looked the same. In other words, despite the best intentions of the sellers and despite the sellers' efforts to "sell value," the buyer could find only one clear differentiator: price.

• Despite this apparent similarity, the customer in these transactions did not select the lowest-price offering.

It was our contention that if this seemingly odd behavior by the customer could be understood, these transactions offered a perfect opportunity to discover what customers meant when they reported receiving "value." Why else would these customers do something so seemingly illogical? Why would they pay more to receive a product or service when a competitor offered the same product or service for less? Most readers will find that the answer is compelling and that it changes the current definition of "sales excellence." And moreover, they will realize that today's seller can take these findings and convert them to strategies and tactics to escape the price-driven sale and thus sell at a premium. They will realize that these skills are teachable, repeatable, and measurable.

THE GENESIS OF CLIENT INSIGHT

At its simplest, the customers in our research reported that they were willing to forego price concerns when, in the buying process, they experienced one or more of the four scenarios that we deem insights that create value. We call these the "Client Insight Creators." That is, these customers were willing to pay a premium, redefine the buyer-seller relationship, erect barriers to the seller's competitors, and establish the seller as a trusted adviser under the following circumstances:

1. The seller revealed to the buyer an *Unrecognized Problem* that the buyer or the buyer's organization was experiencing.

2. The seller established an *Unanticipated Solution* for the buyer's problems that the buyer or the buyer's organization was experiencing.

3. The seller created or revealed an *Unseen Opportunity* for the buyer or the buyer's organization.

4. The seller served as more than just a vendor of products and services but instead served as a *Broker of Strengths*. Specifically, the seller served to make available to the buyer the full range of capabilities of the seller's organization in such a way that these capabilities contributed to an expansion or redefinition of the customer's success. At the individual level, this meant cross-selling.

In the diagram in Figure 1.3, you will see how we have arranged the exploration of the Client Insight Creators in this book. In Part 1, we shall look at the Unrecognized Problem and the Unanticipated Solution, which are hallmarks of modern consultative selling. The definition of "consultative selling" has gone through a

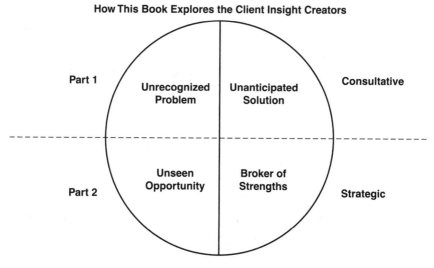

Figure 1.3

fundamental change—indeed, a complete metamorphosis—such that the tactics that worked for you before are likely losing their effectiveness. We're going to explore why that is so and arm you to counteract the trends. We define these two Client Insight Creators as "consultative" because they are primarily practiced at lower and mid-levels of management. They are crucial but chiefly tactical in nature.

In Part 2 of the book we shall look at the Unseen Opportunity and the Broker of Strengths (which is essentially cross-selling when done on the individual level). These two Client Insight Creators require all of the skill of a practiced consultative seller but take the skill level a step higher to the strategic level. For the purpose of clarity, we are defining "consultative" as primarily sales to lower and midlevels of management, and "strategic" as primarily sales to the senior executive level, which includes the hallowed halls of the C suite. Indeed, when we use the terms "executive-level management" and "senior management," we are referring to the C suite and those close to it. Success can be achieved at both the consultative and strategic levels.

Analysis of effective selling has shown unequivocally these four Client Insight Creators at play. And although they can rightly be described as both science *and* art, they have rules that can be learned, practiced, coached, and mastered.

Let's now begin our journey into selling effectively in the twenty-first century—and thereby escaping the price-driven sale—by looking at the Unrecognized Problem.

KEY POINTS

☞ With the advent of the Internet, customer attitudes toward buying (and toward salespeople) have changed drastically. In many cases, salespeople have become obsolete.

This is primarily due to the ever-increasing availability of information.

☞ Customers today don't want sellers to simply talk about their products or services; they can find out that kind of information on a Web site, with the help of an Internet search engine.

☞ Customers are now more sophisticated and will pay a premium for insight, analysis, and expertise that they cannot get anywhere else but from the sales experience.

☞ The Value Equation, to which most Econ 101 students would subscribe, is this:

$$Value = Benefits - Cost$$

☞ The customer's world has drastically and irrevocably changed, and the salesperson's world has not kept up. The customer no longer needs the salesperson to give product or service information because all the information the customer could possibly want is available via the Internet.

☞ Customers will not tolerate being patronized because they no longer recognize the salesperson as the expert.

☞ In the early twenty-first century, sellers will not be successful if they communicate only value. Sellers have to create value by providing insight. There are specific skills, which we call "Client Insight Creators" that have been proven to be successful in differentiation.

☞ Summary of Client Insight Creators:
1. The seller revealed to the buyer an Unrecognized Problem that the buyer or the buyer's organization was experiencing.
2. The seller established an Unanticipated Solution for the buyer's problems that the buyer or the buyer's organization was experiencing.

3. The seller created or revealed an Unseen Opportunity for the buyer or the buyer's organization.

4. The seller served as more than just a vendor of product and services, but instead served as a Broker of Strengths. At the individual level, this meant cross-selling.

| Unrecognized Problem | Unanticipated Solution |
| Unseen Opportunity | Broker of Strengths |

DISCOVERING THE UNRECOGNIZED PROBLEM

To understand is to perceive patterns.

—ISAIAH BERLIN, *Historical Inevitability*

THE PATTERN OF PROFIT

Pattern recognition is the essence of value creation. The ability to help a customer (we use the term "customer" throughout the book to mean both prospective and current clients and customers) assemble existing data in such a way that patterns emerge and problems, solutions, and opportunities present themselves in clear forms is the ability to profitably win business and keep it. Remember that it is not necessarily new information that the customer wants; it is clarity on information that is readily available but may require several lines of sight.

Look at the image in Figure 2.1 for a moment. Does a pattern emerge? What if I were to ask you if you see a cowboy? Do you see it yet? What if I ask whether you see a cowboy riding a pinto? Does the picture begin to come clear, to make sense? So it is with the patterns of problems, solutions, and opportunities in your company. You have in your line of sight a vast array of data points, but until somebody asks

Figure 2.1
Courtesy Rupert Sheldrake, republished from his insightful book *A New Science of Life* (Rochester, Vt.: Park Street Press, 1995).

the right questions, the pattern made by the data points remains unseen. It is as though we were looking at the back of an intricate tapestry (all snarls and knots and strands). We may be able to make out a vague outline of the picture, but until someone shows us the front of the tapestry, it remains somewhat elusive, a bit mysterious.

THE NEW FRAME OF REFERENCE

The new era of buyer-controlled selling has changed the frame of reference for sellers. And actually, "frame of reference" is the perfect metaphor. You may remember that Einstein said that your frame of reference is what determines your experience of time. Well, that's exactly what we're talking about: for the buyer, five minutes spent with an uninformed or ill-equipped salesperson is like two hours of wasted effort. The old-school salesperson who "pitches product" is simply in a different frame of reference. Time, for the buyer, will drag relentlessly. The customer doesn't have time to waste. We're under a great deal of pressure, and we have much to do. Unless we're instantly engaged (or at least very quickly engaged) in something about which we're thinking to ourselves, "Wow, this fellow actually knows stuff that I need to understand . . . about my market, about my company, about my particular performance," time slows to a veritable crawl. Quite literally.

So it is with problems in our business that remain beyond our perception; they are hidden from us; we want some light shed on them. We need, if you will, a learned opinion. For they are and will remain unrecognized until the skillful salesperson, who deals in the subtleties of implications, questions us carefully enough to allow us to discover for ourselves those troubles that mock us silently. Again, it's about pattern recognition. It's about seeing the front of the tapestry.

DEFINITION OF THE UNRECOGNIZED PROBLEM

The first question that a salesperson needs to ask himself or herself is this: What do I know from experience to be the types of problems that come up in this particular industry? And which of these problems can I with my product or service (or expertise) solve?

The Unrecognized Problem is any difficulty that needs to be resolved but is unknown. World-class salespeople have always, from time immemorial, intuitively understood that value can be created for their customers by revealing trouble spots—*through careful questioning*. The great thing is to recognize the whirlpool hidden beneath the gentle eddy on an otherwise placid river.

We use the term "Unrecognized Problem" in this sense: it is a state or a source of difficulty that we need to resolve, but we are not fully aware or cognizant of the exact nature of it. Problems come in all shapes and sizes. The problems we are talking about are either states of difficulty, as in "the assembly line has a problem," or sources of difficulty, as in "one trouble after another delayed the job." In other words, a problem may be either inherent or extraneous but it needs to be resolved. The need for resolution is the vital point. Unresolved, the problem cascades and affects, well, the bottom line.

Salespeople are looking for problems that lurk beneath the surface, that are not immediately apparent to the customers. These types of problems may be just at the periphery of the customers' awareness or far outside their frame of reference. The point is that they do not see them. But the problems are there, and they are affecting the bottom line. The great thing is to find them and resolve them; but customers need help. Because these problems escape their notice, they can't fix them. Or perhaps they are vaguely aware of the problems but have no idea of their magnitude, implications, or potential consequences. They may be too close to the problems to see them clearly (like the man with his nose to the leg of an elephant trying to describe the elephant: "an elephant is a tall, gray, scaly pillar"). Or they may simply be operating in a different frame of reference (like the engineer who is at ease in the world of Newtonian physics trying to understand a problem in quantum mechanics). Whatever the reason that problems remain unrecognized, the simple fact remains: if the customers can't see them, they can't solve them.

THE TWENTY-FIRST-CENTURY SALESPERSON

This may sound far-fetched, but the marketplace has made the quantum leap into a new frame of reference. Enter our salesperson. He is a man who has entered the twenty-first century of sales, and he is well equipped to help customers adjust to the new frame of reference. He has a bewildering array of tools to help them, the first of which being the ability to help them discover for themselves the Unrecognized Problem in their business. How does he do it? We shall look at the how-to in a moment. Let us first look at the big picture. What makes him equipped to help customers? What about his profession sets him apart as uniquely qualified to meet their needs? The ability to create value for customers lies at the intersection of the seller's "industry knowledge" and "business acumen"; that is, he understands their industry, and he understands the nature of their business. He knows how particular problems common in their industry influence the bottom line of their business. We call that intersection, as shown in Figure 2.2, the "Value Creation Capability Zone."

Add "questioning skills" to the mix and you have a recipe for genuine customer discovery. At the intersection of these three professional qualities lies what we call the "Customer Discovery Zone," as depicted in Figure 2.3. It is the zone in which all of the salesperson's knowledge and business acumen are honed by his

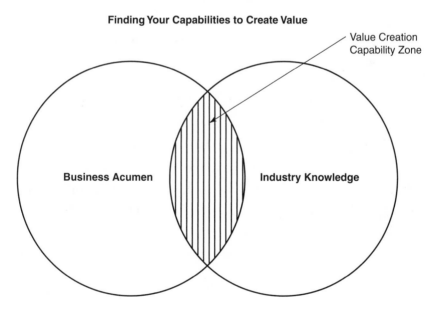

Figure 2.2

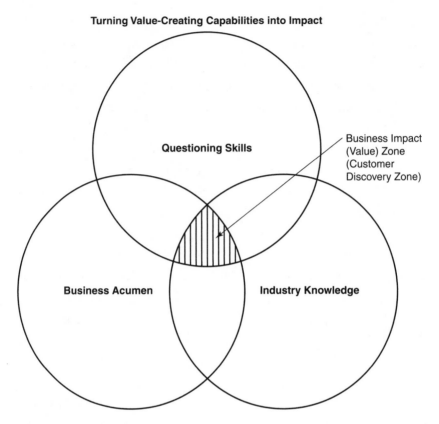

Figure 2.3

questioning skills into a powerful tool. This tool is then used to pry the lid off of an Unrecognized Problem.

The nature of the questioning skills we are talking about needs to be explained a bit. It is not enough to just ask questions. Just asking questions can be very annoying. Most salespeople today would admit the desirability of asking questions, and most would thereby believe themselves to be consultative sellers. But that belief is not well supported by facts. In recent Huthwaite research involving a large number of sales leaders, when asked to describe how their customers perceive them, the leaders indicated that only 4 percent of their salespeople were selling in a way that helped customers see things in a different light. In other words, in the opinion of the executives who employed them, 96 percent of sellers do not create value and/or do not know how to do so using the Unrecognized Problem as a Client Insight Creator.

Asking questions does not make one a consultative seller; asking the right questions at the right time is what makes one consultative. The purpose of questions is twofold:

1. To produce the "aha" reaction from the customer
2. To get the customer to deliver an invitation

It is all about the customer's discovery, and it is intimately related to what we call the "Boundary Conditions," which we shall explore presently. Before we do that, however, let's take a little deeper look at the qualities of a good consultative seller. And by the way, we believe certain things go without saying, so we are not devoting time to them. The first is that the product or service you are selling needs to be excellent, if not superior, just to get in the game. The second is that we assume the salesperson has an intimate knowledge of his or her own products, services, and company capabilities.

Industry Knowledge. Our salesperson is an expert in our industry and understands our competition. He collects knowledge and insight that may be of extraordinary interest to us. He is a walking, talking intelligence brief. His own product or service has forced him to understand the context in which it is used. According to a recent Huthwaite study of Fortune 500 CEOs and SVPs, the top qualification used in selecting a partner is industry knowledge. In fact, 95 percent ranked industry knowledge either first or second on the decision criteria list.

Business Acumen. Our salesperson is a businessperson. It has become incumbent on him to understand not only the intricacies of our industry but also the finer points of our business operations.

He is a man who can make sense of a profit and loss statement. He understands the nature of commercial enterprise (see Chapter 8 for a discussion). He provides insight. We shall discuss this more in Chapter 6, but the key is for the seller to present his offering in terms of business outcome (tangible benefit to the business) and insight rather than in terms of pure differentiation.

Questioning Skills. As we have said, our salesperson is skilled at asking questions such that he can deftly allow us to make our own discoveries and to draw our own conclusions. The fact is that most salespeople are not skilled questioners. On the contrary, research shows that the top skill deficiency among Fortune 100 salespeople is the ability to uncover customer needs! In Chapter 5 we will have a more complete discussion of questioning skills.

These three characteristics make our salesperson exceptionally valuable to us as customers, and we wisely seek his counsel.

SKILLS IN ACTION:
SHOWING THE FRONT OF THE TAPESTRY

Bob Colvin, a friend of ours who sells chemicals, was in South Africa some years ago. As a chemical engineer, he was particularly intrigued by the gold mining processes then being used by Anglovaal (now Metorex) at the New Consort Gold Mines in Barberton. Established in 1885, New Consort is one of the oldest working gold mines in the world.

Gold is extracted from low-grade ore by a cyanide process patented in 1887 and still in use today that was developed by a British metallurgist and chemist named John Seward MacArthur. The rocks are crushed, and then a sodium cyanide solution is allowed to leach through the pile of finely ground rock (the cyanide dissolves the gold), which is then put into a slurry and collected into holding ponds. Nickel acetate is added—to improve gold leaching speed and quantity recovered—by a paddle wheel with cups attached that go into a tank, collect the nickel acetate, and throw it into the trough where the slurry is coming along. And finally zinc dust is introduced, which precipitates the gold out of the slurry.

Well, our inquisitive friend took one look at the cups bearing the nickel acetate, and he realized immediately that those cups had not been cleaned—and this is a material that when the process shuts down will form a crust. So every one of these cups (they were like ordinary small coffee cups) was so corroded and so filled up with crust that it was actually capturing and delivering only half of the amount of nickel acetate needed.

After touring the laboratory, while they were having dinner, the mine manager asked our friend what he thought. Our friend responded with a question of his own:

> "Do you know whether any unprecipitated gold is being left in the sludge after the cyanidation process?"
>
> "I'm not sure," came the hesitant response, "Why do you ask?"
>
> "I was just wondering whether the slurry is getting enough nickel acetate. What might happen if it weren't?" our friend replied.
>
> "Well, I suppose that would slow down the process, and we'd presumably recover less gold."
>
> "Less gold would be precipitated when the zinc dust was added?" our intrepid salesman went on.
>
> "Yes, I suppose so," answered the mine manager, now thoroughly upset.

Our friend assured him that the answer to this very expensive problem was a simple matter of cleaning the cups regularly.

It turned out that this little problem was costing the mine $5 million a year in unprecipitated gold! They ended up having to rework all the sludge, which could have been avoided with the simple observation that the cups were giving half of what they should have held because they weren't kept clean. Now that's creating value by uncovering the Unrecognized Problem.

And that was a very simple problem with a very simple solution. Imagine now the types of complexity that characterize the problems you face in your industry, and remember that you are only imagining the ones you are aware of. What price the hidden problem with unknown and potentially dire consequences?

THE SPiKE MODEL: A RETURN TO THE VALUE EQUATION

From the perspective of the salesperson, helping customers to identify the Unrecognized Problem is a process that has rules that can be learned and put into practice. What did our friend Bob Colvin do? Recall the Value Equation from the first chapter:

$$\text{Value} = \text{Benefits} - \text{Cost}$$

Let's now drill down a little bit, and take a look at how we derive benefits. The equation we use to arrive at benefits is shown in Figure 2.4.

Conveniently enough, this Benefits Equation gives us the acronym SPiKE (skills, process, knowledge, and effort), which is

Figure 2.4

actually a great model for creating value. Let's look at how Bob employed this equation.

Skills

Bob understood that just telling the customer about the problem would have little impact; he knew the customer had to discover the problem for himself. Telling people about their problems just raises hackles, objections, and defensiveness. Because, as we shall see shortly in a discussion of the Boundary Conditions of Communication, people prefer to draw their own conclusions than to be told what they ought to conclude. Bob had the skill to ask the right questions that would guide the customer through either to the "aha moment" or to an invitation (or both). In this case it was the aha moment. Bob didn't accuse the mine manager of running a filthy shop—that would have served no purpose. Rather, he skillfully asked questions to facilitate the manager's own discovery. We will delve into this topic of consultative questioning skills in Chapter 5 and discuss how incisive questions become the key to success.

Process

Bob had gone through a series of teachable, repeatable steps in order to organize his thinking about the industries he was selling into. The process begins with diagnosis that is industry specific. Call together a focus group of your tenured and successful peers, or better yet, some of your key senior management, and brainstorm the industry that you are selling into. Think about the aha moments that your customers have had when the light goes on and they have suddenly recognized a problem they are having. What were the problems? What was the process by which they reached the aha moments? Can it be duplicated with other customers? *From your collective experience*, build a list of the major problems that plague the industry.

The next step is to consider your own company's resources. What problems are you able to solve? What capabilities do you have that map directly to the problems in the industry that you have identified? Put together the list of those problems that you can solve *better than or exclusive from the competition*. The list ought to be pretty short. In fact, if there are more than three or four items on it, you are probably either misinformed about the strengths of your competition or overconfident in your own capabilities. Remember that the flattening of the world has pretty much leveled the playing field; your competition can duplicate much or even most of your capabilities, regardless of the industry in which you live and move and have your being.

Having compiled the list and vetted it for accuracy and given it a serious reality check (apply heat, boil it down), it is time to work out the business effects or consequences of these few problems. How do these problems affect the bottom line? What is likely to happen if the problems remain unrecognized? Given free rein, how will the problems impact the business in question?

Knowledge

Bob was able to credential himself with insight and industry knowledge, gaining him valuable credibility with this customer. As a chemical engineer, he has been trained to understand the systems and processes used in most of the industries that he sells into. But Bob is a learner too. He uses every interaction with a customer as an exchange of insight for learning (we shall look at this exchange in Chapter 9), which he then adds to his knowledge base. He is always expanding his understanding of the companies and industries that make up his customer base. In this case, he was able to use his knowledge of the cyanidation process to uncover extraordinary value for the customer.

Effort

Finally, Bob understood the multiplying power of effort in the value creation process. It is one thing to have the skills, process, and knowledge to be a good salesperson—they are vital tools. But it is effort that brings them into play. Bob could have wandered around the gold mine with blinders on, paying no attention, just waiting for a moment when he could display his wares. Instead, he paid careful attention, scrutinized the process, and made the effort to bring all of his knowledge to bear, and it paid off. He noticed something that had not been previously noticed by anyone else. People no doubt wandered through the mine constantly, but no one had made the effort to pay such careful attention to the cyanidation process. His extra effort gave him serious credibility and leverage with the mine manager. When it came time to discuss his products, there was no negotiation on price. He was able to sell at a premium because he had already created tremendous value for the customer. Just as a side note, Bob worked for a company that believed in motivating its salespeople. He was well coached, and he was handsomely rewarded for success in his compensation package. This enabled him to sell confidently and professionally.

THE BOUNDARY CONDITIONS
OF COMMUNICATION

Considering Bob's success, revealing the Unrecognized Problem may sound like a pretty straightforward way to be successful in sales, right? Not so fast. The most common mistake made by salespeople today is to jump in with solutions before the customer has developed a clear need to solve the problem. In our recent survey of over 600 Fortune 500 sales managers, 72 percent of them said that their salespeople jump in with a solution before the customer has seen a need for one.

Questions are the purest way to assist in pattern recognition and thus the discovery of the Unrecognized Problem. There are actually two very specific reasons for this, which come from behavioral psychology research into cognitive biases. We call them the "Boundary Conditions of Communication." Specifically, they arise from what is known as the "Confirmation Bias":

1. People value what *they say* and their own conclusions more than the value what *they are told.*
2. People value what *they ask for* more than what is *freely offered.*

In other words, as a customer, I would always value the conclusions I draw—with the assistance of guiding questions—more than I would value answers that are shoved down my throat. To tell me what I need as a customer—and how you, as a salesperson, can help me get there—is to fail in the modern selling environment. I will always rather work out for myself what I need and how you can help me get there, but I may need the humble assistance of a salesperson who asks the right questions that help me to see clearly for myself. So by all means ask me questions, but be sure they are helpful and insightful. As we saw in the first chapter, I don't want to be filling in the gaps in your knowledge; I want you to help me structure my thinking and see patterns that were previously shrouded in fog. I want your questions to lead me down the path of my own discovery.

Early in the relationship, the questions asked by the seller are of vital importance. They provide the framework for pattern recognition by the buyer. The seller is doing most of the questioning

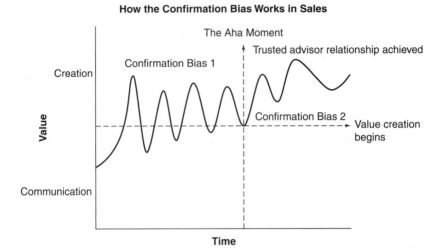

Figure 2.5

and occasionally creating value (using the Client Insight Creators) with insights that keep the buyer engaged and grateful. These are the peaks in the graph shown in Figure 2.5. The valleys are the necessary questions that the seller must ask to fully understand the customer's situation. They fall below the dotted line of value creation because, while important to the seller, they are generally boring and of little interest to the customer.

Once the customer has had the aha moment and has stated a specific want or desire, the customer does most of the questioning. The customer is now seeking advice and expertise, and the seller is able to create more and higher value in the context of Confirmation Bias 2 ("people value what *they ask for* more than what is *freely offered*"). As depicted in Figure 2.5, the peaks represent ever greater discovery by the customer; the valleys show those times when the seller asks insightful questions that lead the customer to ask questions in response. It has been said that one knows one is genuinely a consultative seller when the customer begins responding to questions with a thoughtful pause and then a question of his or her own.

Let's look at how the Confirmation Bias works in sales as shown in Figure 2.5. The vertical axis is labeled "value." This describes the value that is characteristic of the sales process. Low value is considered "value communication." In other words, communicating value (that is, peddling products or services) is of low value in the process. High value is considered "value creation." In other words, creating value (that is, exploring Unrecognized Problems, discovering Unanticipated Solutions, or uncovering Unseen Opportunities within the framework of the Boundary Conditions of Communication) is of high value in the sales process. The horizontal dotted line shows where value creation begins on the *communication* to *creation* scale of the value axis. Above this line is genuine and productive dialogue. Below the line lies the underworld of price negotiation.

The horizontal axis is labeled "time." This shows the passage of time in the sales relationship from left to right. The vertical dotted line shows the time in the relationship at which a *previously Unrecognized Problem* is now on the table. It is the moment of awareness, when the customer suddenly sees the hidden problem or the better solution or the potential opportunity. It is the aha moment. In the parlance of value creation, it is the line at which the customer is no longer so much answering questions as asking questions. The top left quadrant is about discovery; the top right quadrant is about awareness.

You will note that Confirmation Bias 1, "people value what *they say* and their own conclusions more than what *they are told*," plays particularly in the top left quadrant. It is the quadrant of high value *before* the moment of customer discovery, before the point of awareness. It is early in the sales process, when questioning and listening skills are of especially critical importance. In this quadrant, the questions are more important to the customer because they are leading him or her down the path of discovery. It is the time during which the customer is recognizing needs; he or she is becoming aware of things he or she didn't know. The customer is drawing his or her own conclusions.

Confirmation Bias 2, "people value what *they ask for* more than what is *freely offered,*" plays most dramatically in the top right quadrant. It is the quadrant of high value *after* the moment of customer discovery. It is the period in the sales process during which the customer is asking most of the questions. As time passes and value is continually created in the sales process, the salesperson gains the status of counselor or trusted advisor. In this quadrant the answers are more important to the customer because he or she is seeking the counsel and expertise of the seller. The customer is now inviting the seller to share his or her knowledge.

All of that is for the most part in the world of value-creating dialogue, above the horizontal dotted line. Let's look for a moment at what happens in the netherworld below the line. In the bottom left quadrant, the seller is trapped in "oldthink." It is the quadrant characterized by *describing*: describing products or services, describing company attributes, describing 'til you're blue in the face. It is boring for the customer, whose mind will tend to wander in one of two directions (or both):

1. I really, honestly, don't care.
2. Gosh, that sounds expensive.

Obviously this is not a desirable place for either participant to be. In the bottom right quadrant, the seller is playing the price game. She's discounting. Once the customer has recognized the problem and has become determined to do something about it, his only concern now is price. He has gained nothing from the sales experience; no new insight, no new discovery, nothing of value.

Why should he be tempted to pay more than the absolute minimum available? The seller in this bottom right quadrant is allowing the discussion to be all about cost—because she has nothing else to offer. It is the seller's worst nightmare.

Below the value creation dotted line, in short, it's all about price, all the time. In the bottom left quadrant, the seller is actually creating objections. And in the bottom right quadrant, the seller is fighting a price war of her own creation because she's created all those objections and has nothing to offer in terms of insight. So the only thing left for her to do to differentiate and win the business is to give stuff away for free or to lower her price.

This is not to say that the seller up above the line doesn't ever have to negotiate or that the seller up top gets no objections: she does. But by providing the Confirmation Bias as the framework around which she's creating value, the customer is discovering the value for himself and voicing the value for himself and is therefore likely to pay a premium. From a world of *objections* and *discounting*, the value-creating salesperson is moving up into a world of *agreement* and *margin*.

THE CONFIRMATION BIAS IN ACTION

Let's look at some examples of what each of these quadrants look like. As depicted in Figure 2.6, the dot in the top left quadrant represents Jill, a value-creating consultative salesperson early in the sales process. The dot in the top right quadrant is Jack, a value-creating salesperson late in the sales process. The dot in the bottom left quadrant represents Harold, a seller trapped in oldthink. And the dot in the bottom right quadrant is Maude, battling it out in a price war of her own making.

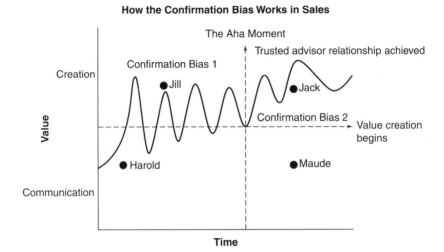

Figure 2.6

Jill the Attorney

Let's imagine that Jill is an attorney. Because she has spent a lot of time in the business and has dealt with a host of customers, Jill has a pretty good understanding of the kinds of problems that are likely to face her customers. One problem in particular is almost always an issue, and she has found that customers are rarely aware of it. The estate tax rate—the rate of tax applicable to a person's estate upon death—is ordinarily somewhere between 45 percent and 49 percent. In other words, upon death, nearly half of a person's estate will be paid to the federal government. If the person dies without any descendants, this isn't a major issue. But for people who are leaving behind children, grandchildren, siblings, or other loved ones, this tax payment is literally money out of their pockets.

Thankfully, this estate tax issue is not relevant to surviving spouses because the U.S. tax code recognizes an unlimited marital deduction: a spouse may transfer an unlimited amount of assets, tax free, to his or her spouse whether during life or upon death. In addition, every U.S. citizen is automatically entitled to a personal exemption against the estate tax, which allows the individual to transfer a certain amount of money to his or her heirs free of estate taxes. Under the legislation signed by President Bush in June 2001, the precise amount of this personal exemption varies from year to year, but generally speaking, it ranges from $1 million to $3.5 million. In other words, if utilized properly, these personal exemptions offer a meaningful shelter from estate taxes.

However, most people do not utilize their personal exemptions properly because the estate tax is a problem they don't even know about. For example, most married couples title their assets in "joint tenancy"—in other words, both spouses appear on the deed to the house, the checking account, the brokerage account, and so on. When the first spouse dies, because the assets are in "joint name," the assets automatically pass to the surviving spouse. Because of the unlimited marital deduction, no estate tax is due. But because there were no assets in the person's estate upon death, no assets were sheltered from estate taxes either. When the surviving spouse dies, any assets in excess of the then-in-existence personal exemption amount will be subject to the hefty estate tax, thus leaving less money behind for survivors. But with proper estate planning, these assets likely could have been sheltered, thereby doubling the total inheritance for surviving loved ones.

It's a problem Jill comes across fairly regularly, and few people are aware of it. Just a few carefully crafted questions by Jill and customers are fairly racing to sign her up as their attorney.

Jack the Rigger

Jack is a salesman for Barnhart Crane & Rigging Company. The company's business is providing innovative solutions to complex

lifting and transportation challenges faced by heavy industry—
from power generation to petrochemical to renewable energy, and
beyond. Jack is dealing with a customer late in the sales process.
He begins the process by asking a lot of questions around the implications of using the solution offered by 95 percent of the industry: a crane with a long boom. The customer has the aha moment
when he realizes that by the traditional method, the company will
have to remove a factory wall and shut down operations for an
intolerable length of time.

Jack offers a solution that will bypass the problems (both re-
moving a factory wall and shutting down operations). He offers
Barnhart's unique Modular Lift Tower, which is like a giant Erec-
tor Set. It has a small footprint, almost limitless configuration
options, and tremendous lift capacity. This unique capability
solves the previously Unrecognized Problems for the customer,
who then begins asking questions about other lifting and transportation challenges that the factory is experiencing. Jack has become a counselor and an advisor simply because he is able to lead
the customer through a process of discovery to the conclusion that
the problems associated with the traditional crane model (a) exist
and (b) are unacceptable.

Harold the CPA

Harold, in the bottom left quadrant, is not having much luck in
this sale. Harold is a CPA specializing in nonprofit tax problems—
and he is very good at what he does. What he's not good at is selling his services. He'll tell you he's an accountant—and a good
one—not a d-mn salesperson (he has long equated selling with
used cars, and he does not favor used-car salespeople). Unfortunately his bias against selling is harming his business.

When talking to the customer, he is preaching. "Here's your
problem." And he unwisely, if not rather pompously, says, "You

don't understand the intricacies of the tax code. You are losing lots of money to Uncle Sam every year because you have no knowledge of the many loopholes for nonprofits. I can help. I have years of aggregate understanding, and what's more, I keep up with every jot and title of the tax code." All the customer keeps thinking is, "Gosh, this guy must be awfully expensive. Doesn't he realize we operate on a shoestring?" Poor Harold is not making headway. Indeed, he is setting up a firestorm of objections.

Maude the Industrial Belts Salesperson

And then there is Maude. She sells industrial belt drives for a large belts, hose, and hydraulics company. It is an admittedly difficult job because industrial belt drives are not just perceived to be a commodity—they are a commodity. Her polyurethane belt drives are durable, functional, and low maintenance—meaning that lifetime costs are exceptionally low. But Maude does not focus on the life-of-ownership costs and the fact that belt drives, which may represent 1 percent of total machinery costs, actually impact up to 60 percent of the machine (a common unrecognized problem). Instead, Maude finds herself trapped in a price negotiation. Her prices are no better (or worse, really) than her competitors'—but discounting will have a detrimental effect not only on margins but also on reputation. Had she been able to ask the types of questions that would have enabled the customer to discover his own issues early in the sales cycle, she would not now be in this position of defending herself in a commodity price war.

Information versus Insight

What are Jill and Jack doing to achieve trusted advisor status and, by the way, sell profitably? They are creating value by leading their

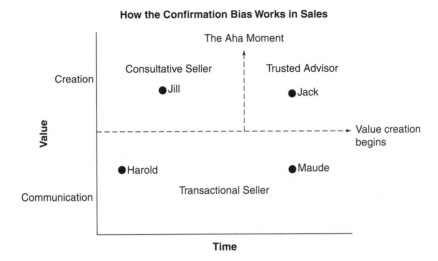

Figure 2.7

customers to the discovery of Unrecognized Problems through careful questioning. The key to helping customers discover the Unrecognized Problem lies in understanding the difference between *information* and *insight*. Information in the modern age, as we have seen, can be gleaned easily and quickly by customers; they don't need a salesperson to tell them anything about products or services. What Jill and Jack bring, and any seller needs to bring, is insight and experience. The seller has a wide range of experience with a broad array of customers, and he or she is able to anticipate the problems that are likely to plague his or her customers—unbeknownst to them. He or she sees things in the marketplace on a regular basis and is able to discern common errors and problems that are rarely seen by customers who work in a stove-piped environment. (See Figure 2.7.)

Preparing for the Aha Moment

As life carries on, a customer may feel pretty confident that all is as it should be. He may become complacent, resting on his laurels.

It is in this complacency that an aha moment may jolt him into action. If a salesperson arrives with a message of potential danger on the horizon, the customer is apt to sit up and take notice. He is apt to be rather grateful and to elevate the salesperson to the rank of counselor. He is apt to consider his salesperson a "Value Creator." By acting as a harbinger of the Unrecognized Problem, his salesperson has created significant value for him. Price is no longer a key differentiator. Salesperson expertise has trumped price. A commodity sale has become profitable, and the customer gains valuable insight that is worth its weight in gold.

Let us now take a look at bringing strategy down to tactics in terms of deliberately incorporating the Unrecognized Problem into your sales repertoire. Look at the industry you sell into. What are the problems that are blatant and that everyone does seem to recognize? (The "everyone" of course refers to every customer, not every seller). For example:

- In the insurance industry, most of the insureds in the world are aware that they have certain loss risk; most of the insureds in the world have a rudimentary understanding of the impact of some sort of loss. Whether that's from being sued, from business interruption, or from the cost of a fire, most of them understand that there is risk.

- Most doctors who use some form of medical product are aware that there's a risk of infection. And they understand that infection prevention is a very important part of performing an operation, especially one that puts some kind of a prosthetic inside of a patient.

- Most people who buy software services understand that there is an issue with both integration with existing software and the adaptability of the new technology. These are things that most of them know.

There are problems in every industry that you can count on the customer to know. Start by saying to yourself, "What am I fairly confident that the customer I'm about to see understands about his or her issues?" List those issues and then put them aside. You need to be aware of them, but you don't want to explore them with the customer—which is what most of your competitors do. How differentiating would it be to bring them to your customers' attention? What happens if everybody that's competing for business works on those obvious problems? Everyone sounds the same; it's a commodity world. So just because you're working on problems (which is what selling has been all about for the past 15 years), don't reassure yourself that you're being a consultative seller.

The first thing you want to think about is what kinds of problems the customers call you in to solve—those problems that they're perfectly aware of, that everyone is perfectly aware of. Indeed, your own marketing department is keenly aware of those types of problems, and they describe in the loftiest ways how you deal with those problems. This is actually why most sellers also talk in rather lofty terms about all of the obvious things that buyers are dealing with. And this is also why most sales efforts deteriorate into price wars. Just asking questions about problems does not differentiate in the modern world; it is just more elaborate commoditization.

From the perspective of the obvious then, what is the larger set of problems that these customers may be experiencing that neither they nor your competitors recognize? What you need to assemble now is that list of potential problems that customers don't seem to be aware of—the Unrecognized Problems. You already have customers. Indeed, undoubtedly you have some who are paying a premium for the value you bring to the table. They are your best customers. They do not harp on price. Why not? Consider whether you have brought an Unrecognized Problem to their attention. What are the other problems you have helped your customers discover in the past? Collect those problems that occur regularly in the industry but that for whatever reason are not generally known. Prepare a tool that will help you to plan your future calls based on the Unrecognized Problems that you have arrived at from experience. This tool should be a matrix that maps generally Unrecognized Problems to the solutions you provide. This matrix will serve you well if you habitually update it and keep your finger on the pulse of the industry. In Part 3 of this book ("Execution"), we will explore in detail how to create the aha moment using questions derived from the material discussed here.

KEY POINTS

☞ Pattern recognition is the essence of value creation. The ability to help a customer assemble existing data in such a way that patterns emerge and problems, solutions, and opportunities present themselves in clear forms is the ability to profitably win business and keep it.

☞ The new era of buyer-controlled selling has changed the frame of reference for sellers.

☞ *Definition of the "Unrecognized Problem."* The Unrecognized Problem is any difficulty that needs to be resolved but is unknown to the customer.

☞ *The twenty-first century salesperson.* The ability to create value for a customer lies at the intersection of the seller's industry knowledge and business acumen; in other words, he understands the customer's industry and he understands the nature of the customer's business. He ties them together with his questioning skills.

☞ The SPiKE model is an expansion of the Value Equation Value = Benefits − Cost, where benefits (which accrue to the customer) = (skills + process + knowledge) × effort.

☞ The Boundary Conditions of Communication (Confirmation Bias), which are critical components to successful sales, are these:

1. People value what *they say* and their own conclusions more than what *they are told*.

2. People value what *they ask for* more than what is *freely offered*.

☞ The key to helping customers discover the Unrecognized Problem lies in understanding the difference between information and insight.

Unrecognized Problem	Unanticipated Solution
Unseen Opportunity	Broker of Strengths

IDENTIFYING THE UNANTICIPATED SOLUTION

If you find a good solution and become attached to it, the solution may become your next problem.

—Dr. Robert Anthony

HELP them chart a better path to an outcome, or achieve a better outcome.

Again we face that curiously powerful type of genius we call "pattern recognition." It is a form of induction that allows us to infer a generality from particulars. As we hone our pattern recognition skills, we will be able to help our customers discover new and better approaches to dealing with problems; we will help them find the Unanticipated Solutions that optimally meet or, better yet, exceed their requirements.

Gaze for a moment at the picture in Figure 3.1. Admittedly, it doesn't look much like a picture at first glance. It is a hodgepodge of black and white particulars, but in it, can you see the general pattern? Do you see a couple of people? Could they be dressed in formal attire and doing the tango? Ah yes, now the pattern emerges because we know what we are looking for. A few carefully chosen questions have sparked our inductive reasoning and, lo and behold, the picture is clear.

Figure 3.1

Courtesy Rupert Sheldrake, republished from his insightful boo*k A New Science of Life* (Rochester, Vt.: Park Street Press, 1995).

DEFINITION OF THE UNANTICIPATED SOLUTION

So it is with the Unanticipated Solution. The customer has a clear and present need and has charted a course to a desirable outcome. But her solution may not be optimal. The job of the salesperson is to either help her chart a better course or achieve a more desirable outcome. When we talked about the Unrecognized Problem, we were trying to get the customer to discover or redefine a problem; when we talk about the Unanticipated Solution, we are trying to get the customer to redefine the connective tissue between the problem and the outcome—or redefine the outcome.

In an effort to be very clear about what we mean by the "Unanticipated Solution," let us must make certain baseline assumptions:

1.   The customer is aware of the need, and feels the pain.

2.   The customer has some general idea of a solution to the problem.

3.   The customer is clear on the desired outcome.

That is to say, the customer has a need—glaring and obvious; explicit and immediate. The customer understands the problem clearly and has decided not only to do something about it but has already taken steps to chart a solution. She knows what is wrong, what she wants to achieve, and how she wants to achieve it. This is not always so cut-and-dried, and in the real world there may be variations on the theme. But the principles hold, and these assumptions best illustrate the nature of the Unanticipated Solution.

The salesperson who can bring about an Unanticipated Solution is the one who can look at the specifications the customer has drawn up and chart a better path to the outcome (better may be cheaper, faster, handsomer, or something else) or he can chart a path to a better outcome (more robust, more profitable, and so on). The twenty-first-century salesperson, who can make sense of a balance sheet and has a degree of business acumen, can read the specifications with one eye always on the outcome. He can determine when a specification is excellent and, more to the point, when it is not. He brings his expertise to bear and charts the superior course. And he discovers to his delight that the customer is willing to pay handsomely for his insight.

So the customer has a problem and an outcome, and she has specified a solution or path to achieve that outcome. She is now in the process of finding a vendor that can meet her specs and deliver the outcome. Figure 3.2 depicts what typically happens.

As you can see, the customer has defined not only the outcome but also the path she has chosen to get there. That's common, especially in larger organizations in which managers will define their

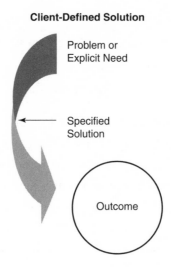

Client-Defined Solution

Problem or
Explicit Need

Specified
Solution

Outcome

Figure 3.2

problem, specify the solution, and then pass it off to purchasing to make the acquisition. Purchasing then carves off differences between providers, making everyone look the same, and then it buys the lowest-cost offering. Most sellers interact with a customer who has already defined what she wants to buy as the method of solving a problem or need and who is therefore telling the seller what she wants. That's all well and good if you want to stay in the transactional space. But there is a better path, as shown in Figure 3.3.

The value-conscious salesperson arrives with the better path or the better outcome. That is to say that the problem is the same but the salesperson provides a better solution leading to a greater outcome. For example, as Coca-Cola looked for ways to increase sales in the late 1980s and early 1990s, McDonald's was looking to offer better value to customers. McDonald's problem was decreasing margins on burgers. The highest margins available were on French fries and Coke. In 1991, at the suggestion of their Coca-Cola salesman, McDonald's introduced the Extra Value Meal, which

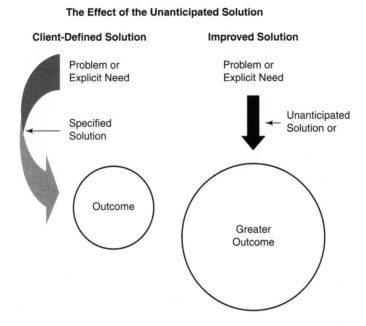

Figure 3.3

encouraged customers to buy French fries and a Coke with their burger for a special price. Sales of Coke at McDonald's rose dramatically that summer. Notice how much larger the outcome is on the right as compared to the left.

With business acumen and solid questioning skills, you have the ability to help the customer rethink her current value proposition. In the case of the Unanticipated Solution, questioning skills are used to provoke an invitation for the salesperson to describe the better path or the better outcome. Business acumen is weighted particularly heavily in the realm of the Unanticipated Solution for the simple reason that every commercial enterprise, in any industry, operates on the same basic principles. The overlap between the salesperson's industry knowledge and business acumen, shown in Figure 3.4, is used to develop a dialogue that will guide the

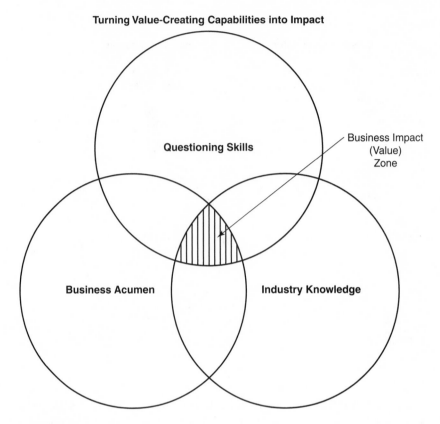

Figure 3.4

customer into asking for an alternative solution and into inviting the salesperson to describe an alternate reality.

DEVELOPING THE
UNANTICIPATED SOLUTION

Business Acumen

As we said a moment ago, every commercial enterprise is run on the same foundation of financial measures. This business taxonomy is the following:

Revenue	How much money did the company generate in sales?
Cost of Sales	What did it cost the company to generate that revenue?
Margin	How much money is the company making from what it's selling?
Expense	What does it cost to run the business?
Profit	What does the company put in its pocket?

General Motors is fairly complicated, and your dry cleaner is pretty straightforward, but despite the differences in their size and global sprawl, they operate on the exact same foundation. Management cares about those five components: revenue, cost of sales, margin, expenses, and profit. Theoretically, everyone in the organization cares about one or more of these fundamentals. Shareholders are concerned chiefly with profits. The CEO of course cares deeply about all five, and they are all on her radar screen. The vice president of sales focuses chiefly on the top three items: revenue, cost of sales, and margin. The chief operating officer is probably most concerned with expenses. The salesperson is primarily interested in margin as his compensation is likely based on some percentage of the margin he generates. In other words, everyone cares about his or her part of the P&L statement.

For our purposes here, it is enough to understand that all business outcomes affect one or more of these five components of business acumen. It is therefore incumbent on the salesperson who seeks to identify the Unanticipated Solution to understand these principles and to be intimately familiar with how his product or service can impact any or all of them. The essence of the Unanticipated Solution is a better outcome, which will have its impact on one or more of these financial measures.

Take, for example, a company that believes that because there has been a steadily increasing rate of travel expenditures by its personnel, it now needs to do something to control the cost of travel. What would the typical good manager do? He would organize a request for proposals (RFP). He would spec it out. And it would have a single line of sight: Reduce the cost of travel. Suppliers vying for the business would be required to provide information about their size, companies they've worked with, and success stories. It's all very predictable.

The salesperson who responds by trying to shave pennies here and there off the cost of travel—by getting an extra ½ percent off from some hotel chain, a little bit off in terms of airline and rental car prices, and then making some sort of statement about per diems—is playing the transactional game. You don't really need a salesperson to do that. You just need a quote machine. Look at the left-hand side of the picture in Figure 3.5: the business impact touches only expenses. And actually, that's how most people respond to RFPs. They accept the premise that the defined solution is optimal to reach the desired outcome.

The sophisticated salesperson, in contrast, seeks a dialogue with the manager who first noticed that too much money was being spent on travel. In that dialogue, she draws the manager into recognizing that the answer to controlling travel costs may not lie

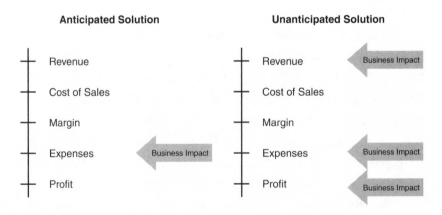

Figure 3.5

in shaving pennies off the line-item expenses after all. Perhaps it lies rather in some form or fashion that touches revenue, and even profit. Perhaps it lies in prebuying—or buying in bulk—room rates and airline miles, and then to the extent that those are not used, selling them on a monthly basis. It may not have an impact on revenue per se but it may generate some offset revenue against the expenses incurred. The right side of the picture above is the "insight" alternative to the obvious cost-cutting strategy of the left side.

Industry Knowledge

In the identification of the Unanticipated Solution, industry knowledge is of a particular type and plays a precise role. The reason that the Value Creation Capability Zone lies only at the intersection of business acumen and industry knowledge (see Figure 3.6) is that

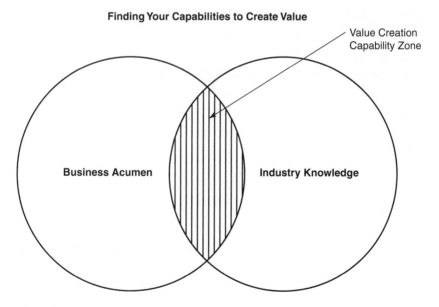

Figure 3.6

the industry knowledge we are talking about must be seen through the lens of the five business fundamentals. In every industry the concerns and vagaries of these principles vary dramatically. Thus the necessity of the overlap.

The industry knowledge that plays here is of a comparative sort; it's about relativity. If you are looking at the consulting industry (or any industry that deals in intellectual property for that matter), for example, and you find that a particular company has substantially lower profits than its competitors, there may be problems in the expense column that ought to be considered.

So the industry knowledge we are talking about is essentially about industry standards and how a particular company is doing vis-à-vis its competitors. It is all about *relative performance*. How is our target company doing when compared to the industry in each of the five categories? Does it compare favorably or unfavorably against the industry average for gross profit margin, for example? Looking at a line item from a popular business database reproduced below, what would you conclude?

Profitability	ADP	Administaff	Ceridian	Paychex	Industry Median
Gross Profit Margin	51.10%	20.50%	45.90%	**66.80%**	52.60%

Courtesy Hoover's, Inc. (www.hoovers.com).

Is there a company in the chart above that might benefit from a particular kind of business outcome? And as you can see, you don't have to be an expert in the payroll and tax filing processor industry. Not even knowing much about the industry we're dealing with, we can reach some basic conclusions. How about the auto parts manufacturing industry? What might spark your interest from the following numbers?

Valuation	Johnson Controls	Exide	Lear	Magna International	Industry Median
Price/Sales Ratio (Cost of Sale)	0.51	0.09	0.09	0.38	0.75
Net Profit Margin	3.20%	(6.30%)	(5.90%)	2.80%	4.70%

Courtesy Hoover's, Inc. (www.hoovers.com).

As you can see, we can make astute discoveries about a company by comparing and contrasting it with the industry at large.

Questioning Skills

Recall for a moment the Boundary Conditions of Communication from the last chapter. The second Confirmation Bias states that people value what *they ask for* more than what is *freely offered.* This gives us the frame of reference in which to develop our questioning for the Unanticipated Solution. The object is to craft your questions in such a way that the customer *extends an invitation* for you to deliver your expert opinion and advice—for you to discuss your solution. Again, your solution will have business impact in ways that

---

The Data Say: The biggest consistent skill gap is getting to the real need.

Solutions are offered before the customer states a defined need 63.4 percent of the time.

87 percent of sellers start by asking the customer to define the desired solution.

Sellers are thereby getting customer wish lists—never discovering the real burning business issues.

The Impact Is: A staggering amount of wasted selling time.

For a sales force with 500 salespeople, one 60-minute sales call per day equals 7,000 hours per year wasted.

the customer could not have anticipated without your tactful guidance. It is a solution that will redefine your customer's outcome.

SKILLS IN ACTION: HOW IT'S DONE

Some years ago, a friend of ours was selling for Moore North America (now RR Donnelly), and he had the opportunity to engage with Budget Rent A Car. Budget had a problem: its printing costs were too high. By quite a bit. The company's outcome was obvious: reduce the cost of printing. Its specified solution was to put out a request for a whole bunch of bids and select the cheapest. It seemed to make sense, and frankly it's what many companies continue to do in order to reduce costs. But our friend's sales team came up with a better and indeed, an Unanticipated Solution. As it turned out, it was both an easier path to the outcome and a substantially more profitable outcome.

The Unanticipated Solution he brought was not in fact a reduced print cost for each job. Rather, it was a threefold solution:

1. *Reduction of staff through outsourcing.* It ought to be said that the Unanticipated Solution oftentimes rains on someone's parade. Nobody, for instance, wants to lose his or her job to outsourcing. So, if he had tried to sell to the wrong person, he or she would have thrown him out on his ear.
2. *Incorporation of revenue-generating ideas.*
3. *Creation of an economy of scale.*

Reduction of Staff through Outsourcing

During his investigation he discovered that Budget had several full-time employees (FTEs) in separate departments managing the coordination of the print production process. Our friend offered to put an expert on site. Budget accepted the offer, which allowed it to reallocate precious human resources. The added benefit to Budget was on-site printing expertise that was always available— no more waiting for an internal resource to call the printer and then waiting around for the printer to show up. It not only saved a lot of money but prevented the usual headache.

Incorporation of Revenue-Generating Ideas

One of the things that Budget was very interested in was new ways to drive revenue. So instead of just offering to look at the print costs, our friend actually looked at some of the company's revenue-generating marketing campaigns and brought forward some resources and ideas on how to bring in more potential customers by creative marketing campaigns, use of different lists, and so on. It was a business solution he was able to bring based solely on his experience in the marketplace writ large. Interestingly, having never sold into the car rental industry, he was not strictly familiar with the industry per se. But his marketplace expertise and some focused research paved the way. He rented a couple of cars on his own time, talked to some of the local owners, and got some ideas about what they did and how they did it. He quickly learned the kinds of problems they were experiencing with their headquarters regarding production and distribution. By doing this research, he was able to give Budget some revenue-generating ideas from its printing contractors that it did not expect.

Creation of an Economy of Scale

Had he just bid on what was being offered—the one piece of Budget's print universe—he would have made very little profit on the venture. Instead, our friend offered to take on the whole universe of Budget's print needs, in both the print production and the marketing groups. By doing this, he was able to generate a very profitable economy of scale that would actually be able to lower the company's physical print costs.

Another Unanticipated Solution was his ability to produce value reports. He actually gave Budget monthly line-by-line reports of everything he accomplished, including print cost reductions, economies-of-scale enhancements, revenue-generating ideas that were implemented, and efficiencies that were gained. Prior to this, Budget had had a very sketchy understanding of where it was losing money (and how much) and where it was saving money (and how much). He gave the company an itemized process for quantifying its savings and its losses (which he minimized by implementing new processes).

As he had been properly trained in SPIN (SPIN is a registered trademark of Huthwaite, Inc., 1988; you will read much about SPIN in Chapter 9), he began the selling process by asking two questions. The first was about processes that were inefficient, ineffective, or just plain complicated. The second was along the lines of, "Are you aware of all the costs associated with producing a printed document?" Of course, he knew the answers, but he suspected the company didn't. To answer his question, Budget made the headcount it takes to coordinate printing, to make the phone calls back and forth to the printers—all of the soft costs and reporting challenges.

He noted a particular process that was woefully inefficient; in fact, "nightmare" might not be too strong a word. Earlier, during his research phase, one of the local rental agencies had pulled out a direction card and said, "Look at this thing. It's ugly, it takes forever to get, and it costs a fortune." It turned out that "direction cards" (which, just as it sounds, are printouts of driving directions from the rental agency to any number of local destinations) were being printed individually, and they were expensive, they were a hassle, they were one color, and they looked like mimeograph copies. So he created a print-on-demand shell program (because keeping these cards in stock was one of Budget's toughest processes), whereby he preprinted the company logo in two colors (blue and orange, which are its corporate colors). He then printed directions as needed, in highly efficient-looking black ink, right over the logo—so the cards came out in three colors, and were really quite attractive. He set up a weekly run of only those direction cards that were actually needed at each location. It was extraordinarily efficient and saved the company a bundle.

Another process that was out of whack was procurement, particularly of the rental agreements. Budget spent millions of dollars on these four-part forms that you must fill out when you rent a car. Our friend found that Budget operators were ordering sporadically, and that no way existed for the company to gang the operators' orders (and the more you gang the orders, the more efficient the print process, the more the savings). So he was able to create a gang order process by which automatically, twice a month, gang orders would go to the printer. That reduced Budget's price for the forms, which in turn increased profitability.

His approach wasn't the cheapest, but it changed Budget's entire paradigm for the better. He saved the company the money it was expecting, but he also saved it a lot more money than it would have saved by shaving off little bits on the printing costs by bidding the business out. It wasn't an appeal to how nicely his letters formed up and how beautiful his colors were. It was an appeal to the balance sheet and income statement of a multibillion-dollar company.

FROM CONCEPT TO REALITY: BRINGING THE UNANTICIPATED SOLUTION TO LIFE

Like uncovering the Unrecognized Problem, arriving at the Unanticipated Solution is a process that has rules that can be learned and applied. Let's look at the Budget Rent A Car sale (or perhaps better, partnership) in the context of the Benefits Equation (or SPiKE model):

$$(\textbf{S}kills + \textbf{P}rocess + \textbf{K}nowledge) \times \textbf{E}ffort = Benefits$$

Skills

The chief skills employed here are once again a matter of effective questioning. Questions are used to elicit an invitation to discuss the greater outcome in the context of the impact on the business principles we have discussed. In this case Budget was clear on the desired outcome: reduce the cost of printing. The company's criteria, our friend found out, were fairly straightforward: (1) cheap, (2) high-volume capacity, (3) national coverage, and (4) on-time delivery—in that order. The criteria were fine. It was the hoped-for outcome that was suboptimal.

Having done the research, the first question our friend asked was, "Who pays for personnel in this department?" He was seeking to discover whether personnel came out of the same budget as the print costs. It was a simple background question (a "situation question" in the SPIN vernacular), but it was vital to the investigation. He already knew that Budget had several full-time employees managing the coordination and the print production processes, and he knew that was serious overkill. When the answer turned out to be that yes, in fact these personnel and print costs came from the same budget, it was a short step to the solution.

He asked the value question ("need-payoff," if you're a SPIN afi-cionado) that led to an invitation to discuss his solution: "If we look at the whole pool of money for print costs and employee costs, and if we could reduce both of those, who would benefit and why?"

Remember that the object of questioning skills in this case is to get the customer to invite you to tell him how he can achieve a more significant business outcome than he is currently hoping for.

Process

Delivering the Unanticipated Solution is a four-step process (Figure 3.7):

Step 1. Identify and prioritize areas of business impact.

Step 2. Plan.

Step 3. Elicit invitation.

Step 4. Propose solution.

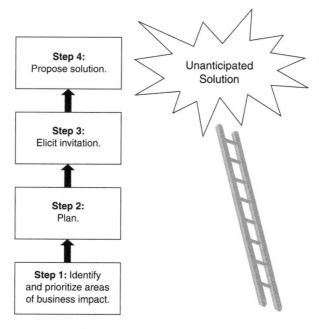

Figure 3.7

Step 1. Identify and Prioritize Areas of Business Impact

In order to identify potential areas of business impact, it is important to do some general industry research within the framework
of the five business fundamentals (revenue, cost of sales, margin,
expense, and profit). Compare your customer company to the
industry in which it operates. Discover inconsistencies, aberra-
tions, and anomalies. Find areas where your customer or prospect
does not conform to industry standards (or compares unfavorably).
Target those areas and try to figure out what solutions you may
have to offer in terms of business impacts.

We've developed an exercise that will help you to identify and
prioritize your list of possible solutions. As you look at Figure 3.8,
you will see on the left "your capabilities." This block is divided
further:

- *Company capabilities.* What outcomes is your company
  capable of producing?

- *Products and/or services capabilities.* What solutions does
  your product or service provide?

- *People capabilities.* Are there individuals in your company
  who can bring special capabilities to bear on behalf of the
  customer?

In this preparation stage, take the time to map these capabilities
to the customer's business functions. These are the same principles
we discussed earlier in the chapter:

- *Revenue.* Can you help generate more money in the customer's sales function?

- *Cost of sales.* Can you lower the cost to generate that income?

- *Margin.* Can you widen the gap between revenue and cost
  of sales?

- *Expense.* Can you lower the customer's cost of doing business?

- *Profit.* Can you affect the proportion of net income?

Perhaps you will find two or three areas where you can positively impact your customer's business. That would be lucky. Do not be disappointed if there is only one or two. That is enough for a genuine value-creating interaction with the customer. In the case of Budget Rent A Car, our friend found three—one related to revenue and two related to cost cutting (expense).

We recommend that you start by filling in the box where the customer *expects* an outcome to impact his or her business and highlight it in some way to distinguish it as the *expectation*. Then fill in the boxes where you can have an impact. Each cell in the chart represents a capability matched to the impact. Figure 3.8 shows what our friend's solutions plan looked like.

Solutions Plan

		Client Business Functions				
		Revenue	Cost of Sales	Margin	Expenses	Profit
Your Capabilities	Company	Generate revenue by bringing new marketing ideas.			Reduce expenses by creating an economy of scale.	
	Products and/or Services				Expectation: Decreased print costs.	
	People				Eliminate 4 FTEs; replace with 1 of ours.	

Figure 3.8

As you can see, he had mapped out some possible solutions that were utterly unanticipated by the customer. He prioritized them as follows: (1) eliminate four FTEs because that would have the largest impact on expenses, (2) create an economy of scale because that would have the next highest return, and finally (3) bring new marketing ideas to improve revenue. As it happened, our friend was able to bring all three to bear in helping Budget identify a completely Unanticipated Solution to its problem. It does need to be said that while all of his hypothesized options came into play, they just as easily may not have. You will not know which solutions to offer until you get into the meeting and ask the questions you will plan out in the next step.

Step 2. Plan

By "plan" we mean work out how you get an invitation to describe your better outcome. What is the logical questioning path you are going to use to elicit the request for you to share your expertise? Having mapped your capabilities to your customer's business functions, it is time to work out the kinds of questions that will lead to that invitation to discuss the path to the outcome or the greater outcome. Particularly if you have more than one or two boxes filled in on the solutions plan, you will need to craft a dialogue that covers all of the bases.

Unlike the Unrecognized Problem, the Unanticipated Solution is rarely determined *a priori*, before you arrive at the meeting with the customer. You simply don't have enough information about the customer. Rather, you will arrive at the meeting armed with a starting hypothesis and work from there. The Unanticipated Solution is worked out *ex post facto*, after you have interacted with the customer long enough to understand the real business issues involved. Your planning session will therefore focus on preparing the kinds of questions that will lead the customer to seek more, to extend the sought-after invitation to share your solution. As we have seen in the solutions plan, you do have to have the ability to connect to the metrics and financials of the customer's business.

In preparing for your meeting, try to come up with a working hypothesis, but remember this is just the starting point. It is not the end point. You will reach the end, and find the optimal solution, during your conversation with the customer. In preparing for the meeting with Budget, our friend had three starting hypotheses. It was a matter of serious call planning to come up with some questions that might lead the customer to ask for solutions. We have already seen the questions our friend asked to get to his customer's top priority, reducing staff and getting one of his own on site. Figure 3.9 shows how he approached the other two.

Finally, in Step 2, you must determine the advance that you seek. An "advance" is where an event takes place, either in the call or after it, that moves the sale forward toward a decision. In this case the advance will be an invitation to describe your solution. Be sure to prepare yourself to recognize the invitation when it comes.

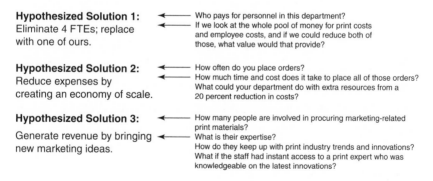

Hypothesized Solution 1: Eliminate 4 FTEs; replace with one of ours.
◄──── Who pays for personnel in this department?
◄──── If we look at the whole pool of money for print costs and employee costs, and if we could reduce both of those, what value would that provide?

Hypothesized Solution 2: Reduce expenses by creating an economy of scale.
◄──── How often do you place orders?
◄──── How much time and cost does it take to place all of those orders? What could your department do with extra resources from a 20 percent reduction in costs?

Hypothesized Solution 3: Generate revenue by bringing new marketing ideas.
◄──── How many people are involved in procuring marketing-related print materials?
◄──── What is their expertise? How do they keep up with print industry trends and innovations? What if the staff had instant access to a print expert who was knowledgeable on the latest innovations?

Figure 3.9

Step 3. Elicit Invitation

The third step in the process is about execution. Everything about your execution as a seller should be in response to cues that you get from the buyer (as opposed to how most sellers sell, which is just by their own drumbeat of activity). Having garnered the important first meeting—and it really doesn't matter how many meetings it takes after that—begin the process of leading the customer to make a discovery. Until there is a conclusion drawn by the customer, wherein she experiences an aha moment, you ought to continue asking the kinds of questions that keep drawing her attention to make connections she isn't making. And remember, these questions occur naturally in a rational dialogue; this is not an interrogation.

Once the customer has drawn the conclusion, the next thing you are looking for is an invitation to describe your solution. Ask your questions as planned, but be sure to listen very carefully to the answers. Be proactive in your selling, but constantly monitor where the buyer is. You do not want to jump in with solutions before you have received an invitation to do so.

Guide the dialogue in such a way that the customer sees you as an expert whose opinion is worthy of consideration. Bring to bear the full weight of your business acumen, industry knowledge, and questioning skills. It is at the intersection of those three talents that you will discover the Business Impact (Value) Zone. That intersection is where you positively affect your own margin while at the same time deliver tremendous value to your customer. Question carefully and pay attention to the responses. When—and only when—you hear the invitation (the advance you had planned for) are you ready for the final step, which is to propose your solution. Again, it may be in the first or it may be in the ninth meeting.

Step 4. Propose Solution

Once you get the invitation, it's time to describe your capabilities. It is time to share your hypotheses. Remember from Chapter 1 that the customer highly values humility. Please don't be haughty or appear triumphant: customers do not want your arrogance. They want your advice, your counsel, your solutions. They will value you as a trusted advisor if you can really show them a better path to heaven or a better heaven. Be sure to describe the solution from an outcome viewpoint (through the lens of the business impact), not through features and functionality.

When you have finished describing your solution, ask the buyer to connect the dots: "So tell me how this solution will benefit your company." When that's done, the table's been set: the customer has drawn her conclusions, she has extended the invitation to describe your solution, you've given a description, and she has at last connected the dots. She sees clearly the benefits of your solution to the problem.

At this point it is time for the formal proposal. At the customer's request (or if she doesn't ask you, ask her permission to), submit a proposal. In great selling, a proposal is simply the memorialization of what has already been agreed to. A lot of sellers make a terrible mistake in letting the proposal do the selling. It never will. Even great sellers, who do a pretty good job of uncovering customer needs and giving the customer an aha moment, when asked to submit a written proposal, tend to revert to the standard template that was put out by the marketing department and that describes the wonderful features of the product. When you propose a solution, be sure to capture the aha the customer experienced and what the customer saw as the benefits. Remember, what the customer says is more valuable than what she is told. So build the presentation around the aha expressed by the customer.

Proposals are never read thoroughly; they're skimmed for the reader's pet preferences. But you can be assured that everyone will look at one page: the pricing page. When it comes to putting your solution on paper, it is important that you cast your proposal in terms of what the customer cares about. Do not rely on your usual boilerplate for proposals. If need be, create a new boilerplate for the Unanticipated Solution; it will need to be extraordinarily customizable. Because as we have said, the proposal just memorializes the deal that's been done. Celebrate *after* the successful implementation of your solution!

Knowledge

Industry knowledge is not quite *as* important in the Unanticipated Solution paradigm, but what knowledge you lack, you should try to make up for in research, homework, and exploration. Do comparative analysis within your customer's or prospect's industry. Discover how your customer compares to the competition. At Moore North America, our friend took a great deal of time studying the car rental industry. He learned a great deal about it before he ever sat down to work through the steps necessary to deliver the Unanticipated Solution. He even visited several car rental agency sites and asked all sorts of questions in order to get as smart as he could as quickly as possible.

What is perhaps most important from a knowledge standpoint is your understanding of your own company's capabilities, your products or services, and the capabilities of the people you have at your disposal. It is vital that you be able to extrapolate from your capabilities to business outcomes. To do that, you need a strong working knowledge of the fundamentals of commercial enterprise and a strong understanding of how your product or service plays in the business context.

Effort

Take skills, process, and knowledge, and multiply them by the effort you put into the cause and you have your benefit to the customer. Effort, otherwise known as "hard work," includes bits from each of the others. It means practicing (with feedback) your questioning skills and carefully planning. It means putting plenty of time into your solution plan, call plans, strategy plans, and other preparation tools. And it means doing your homework. There is no substitute for hard work—and you'll find it's worth the effort.

SKILLS IN ACTION: SELLING THE UNANTICIPATED SOLUTION

As you read through the next couple of stories, see if you can work out how the salespeople involved used the SPiKE model to bring exceptional value in the form of an Unanticipated Solution to their respective customers.

Oakite Products

One of the great stories of selling an Unanticipated Solution is the tale of how Chemetall Oakite ("surface treatment for every industry"), then Oakite Products, won the business at Carrier (the "world leader in heating, air-conditioning, and refrigeration systems"). Carrier had decided that it needed to cut down on its paint costs. Parker Rustproof Corporation had the business, and it was theirs to lose. American Chemical Paint Company and Oakite were invited to the table for what was supposed to be a purely transactional bidding war—the phosphating-prepainting treatment was a straight commodity in the eyes of all but one.

As it happened, it did begin as a price-driven competition. Parker Rustproof, who did not want to appear stingy, agreed to cut down its profit margin and save Carrier approximately $2,000 per year in the phosphating process (this was in the 1940s, when $2,000 was real money). The Parker Rustproof representatives had laid out all of their literature and explained how the price reduction was cutting into their own profits, but they would willingly make the sacrifice to keep the business. American Chemical Paint representatives then came in and did the same: they laid out their literature, explained the processes and the chemical concentrations that were necessary for the phosphating process to work, noted that the chemicals were a fixed-price commodity, and then said that they would be willing to surrender their profit (also a savings of about $2,000 per year for Carrier) to win the business.

Enter Oakite, whose savvy salesman was always on the lookout for the Unanticipated Solution. He had read all of the literature handed out by his competitive predecessors, studied their phosphating process in minute detail, and discovered the winning solution. The literature of his competition showed that the phosphating process was a five-stage process. The first was a cleaning tank (alkali that cleans off the oil and grease), which—like all the rest—ran at 160°F. Next came a rinse (and the rinse tank always had to be overflowing), which also ran at 160°F. Then the third tank, phosphating, ran at 160°F. The fourth tank, a wet rinse, like the others, ran at 160°F. And finally, the fifth tank, which was chromic acid, also ran at 160°F. What the Oakite rep knew that had apparently escaped the others was that you can do a proper rinsing job at room temperature (you gain nothing in the rinsing process by increasing the temperature). So his literature cut the temperature on the rinses out of the equation. Well, as you can imagine, when you have a 10,000-gallon tank with a two-inch pipe constantly overflowing, heating it to 160°F is no small cost. The competition was talking chemicals

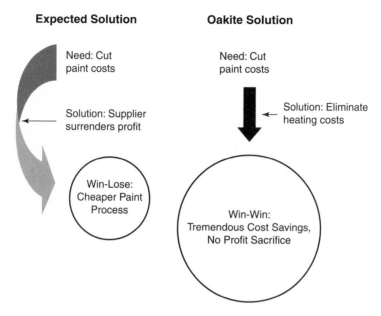

Figure 3.10

and fighting a commodity price war. The Oakite salesman showed Carrier that by eliminating the heat on the two rinse tanks, it would save many thousands of dollars, and he won the business without having to sacrifice on the price of the chemicals (Figure 3.10).

When you do finally meet with the customer, remember that the object is to get the customer to arrive at the solution on his or her own, through careful questioning. It is all very well to know the solution, but to tell it—to offer it up—is to fail. You must ask the right questions.

THE AHA MOMENT

When the buyer ponders the pros and cons of different possible vendors and their solutions to his problems, he is most desperate for that momentous aha moment that will clear the skies and let the sun shine through. You know that moment when you are pondering what seems unfathomable, and suddenly you get clarity? Archimedes, as you may recall, in a fit of jubilation, leapt straight out of the bath and ran naked down the streets shouting "Eureka! I've found it!" We do not necessarily recommend that, but you know what we're talking about.

Employing the Unanticipated Solution takes experience—not in the sense of practice (although there is no substitute for practice) but rather in the sense that the resource comes from your own experience in the marketplace. In other words, absolutely raw, perfectly brand new, fresh-out-of-college salespeople cannot employ Client Insight Creators because they have no marketplace experience to draw on. They could be trained in matters of the marketplace, which we shall consider in Chapter 9, but it would have to be a conscious and heroic training effort. Aside from targeted training, you will be relying on the intuitive ability to connect the dots.

It is a real discipline to learn to extract and codify useful nuggets from your experience, but it is a vitally important discipline. Recognize that every interaction with a customer—other than the transactional customer—whether it is successful or not, and whether you employ a Client Insight Creator or not, yields perhaps one new bit of useful information and adds to your overall experience. Sometimes that experience has nothing to do with the Client Insight Creator, but often it does. So it is important to get into the habit of sitting down periodically to think through and codify your experience. Do not let it ossify.

And remember that both information and experience have a half-life. The market ages. Pretty soon the market catches up to you and understands its world and the changes that have come upon it. So you have to stay fresh. And the way to stay fresh is by thinking back through every time you've employed the Client Insight Creators—consciously or not—and ask yourself what you learned. Think back through every interaction with a customer and every sales opportunity: what did you learn? And does it fall into a category where you gleaned an insight that the market doesn't see yet? Be on constant alert, continually freshening up, habitually codifying your learning. This gives you one of the key tools to escape the price-driven sale.

KEY POINTS

☞ *Definition of the Unanticipated Solution:* Help them chart a better solution or achieve a better outcome.

☞ *Conditions for the Unanticipated Solution:*

1. The customer is aware of the need, and feels the pain.
2. The customer has some general idea of a solution to the problem.
3. The customer is clear on the desired outcome.

☞ The seller's solution must be focused on creating a business impact, or there is no value created for the customer. The Business Impact (Value) Zone lies at the intersection of business acumen, industry knowledge, and questioning skills.

☞ Business acumen is crucial to figuring out how your solution will have positive business impact for the client. The seller must impact one or more of the following five financial measures:

Revenue	How much money did the company generate in sales?
Cost of Sales	What did it cost the company to generate that revenue?
Margin	How much money is the company making from what it's selling?
Expense	What does it cost to run the business?
Profit	What does the company put in its pocket?

☞ It is all about relative performance. Understand your customer's industry vis-à-vis their competitors on the above five financial measures.

☞ Questioning skills are essential for success in positioning the seller's solution. The object is to craft your questions in such a way that the customer extends an invitation for you to deliver your expert opinion and advice—for you to discuss your solution.

TURN CONCEPT TO REALITY

In-depth research, case studies, and diagnostics
www.huthwaite.com/escaping

PART 2

VALUE CREATION AND THE STRATEGIC SELLER

CHAPTER 4

THE ESSENTIALS OF COMMERCIAL ENTERPRISE

Since the purpose of business is to satisfy existing desires,
or stimulate new ones, if everyone were genuinely happy,
there would be no need for business any longer.

—MIHALY CSIKSZENTMIHALYI

THE CONTEXT OF THE EXECUTIVE SALE

Before we turn to the final two Client Insight Creators, first, let's take
a careful look at the differences between consultative and strategic
selling, and second, let's consider the fundamentals of commercial
enterprise. These are important because the Unseen Opportunity and
the Broker of Strengths play largely at the strategic, or executive,
level. And while all four Client Insight Creators are dependent to
some degree on an understanding of the workings of business, the
Unseen Opportunity and the Broker of Strengths are first among
equals because selling at the executive level requires an extraordinary
appreciation of the business of business.

As seen in Figure 4.1, the Unrecognized Problem and the Unanticipated Solution can both be shared across the management spectrum.
Significantly, they are the only two Client Insight Creators that can be
proffered at the purely tactical level at lower levels of management.

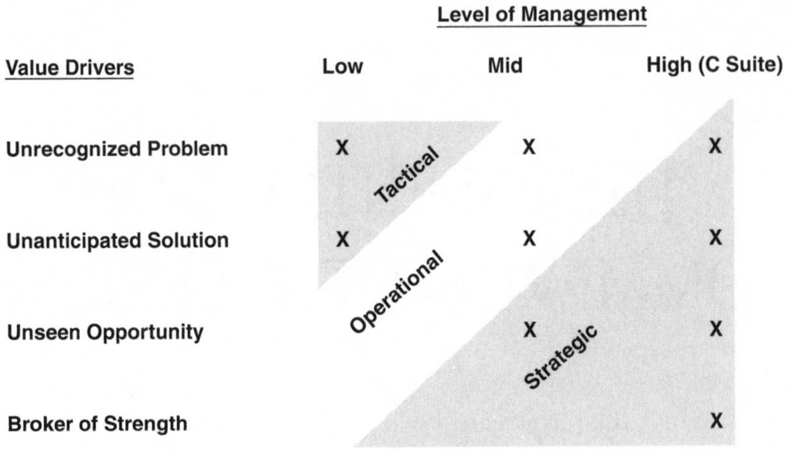

Value Drivers	Level of Management		
	Low	Mid	High (C Suite)
Unrecognized Problem	X	X	X
Unanticipated Solution	X	X	X
Unseen Opportunity		X	X
Broker of Strength			X

(Diagonal regions labeled: Tactical, Operational, Strategic)

Figure 4.1

As we enter the realm of the Unseen Opportunity, we move up into the operational and strategic levels of middle to upper management. It is high-level selling as a general rule. For clarification, we use the term "executive management" to refer to senior management and the C suite.

CONSULTATIVE VERSUS STRATEGIC SELLING

We define "strategic selling" as high-level selling: either selling to executive management or enterprise-to-enterprise selling. "Consultative selling"—while it can take place at every echelon of a corporation—cannot take place with every customer. There are customers at every level of a corporation who are "transactional customers" (those with whom you can never have a strategic or consultative sale). There are also customers who are "nontransactional" at every level of an organization, and those are the ones to whom you can sell either consultatively or strategically, depending on their level.

The Data Say: Salespeople infrequently make the leap from midlevel selling to executive management.

60 percent of the time, salespeople inappropriately leverage the people they have access to in an account. They have the same approach for a focus of receptivity as they do for a focus of power.

The Impact Is: Wasted access to senior management.

Imagine the salaries and compensation of the sales and sales management team of a company equals $150 million. Let's say 500 salespeople each conduct an average of 4 sales calls per month; that's 2,000 per month, which averages then 24,000 calls, say, 25,000 per year. That comes to about $6,000 per call. And that's just the direct costs. Now imagine we wasted 60 percent of it. Your salespeople are wasting $3,600 every time they go out on a call.

Selling high requires a particular depth of awareness of the dynamic that takes place in a free marketplace; consultative sellers can get by with a substantially more superficial understanding. The research shows that most salespeople get it wrong because they don't recognize this difference in context. Take a glance at the research noted in the box above. The "focus of receptivity" was defined as the point in an account where there were receptive people who were prepared to listen sympathetically. The "focus of power" was defined as the elusive point in an account where there were people able to make the decision.

The focus of receptivity. The point in an account where there were receptive people who were prepared to listen sympathetically.

The focus of dissatisfaction. The point in an account where there were people unhappy with the present system or supplier.

The focus of power. The elusive point in an account where there were people able to make the decision.

How does this data affect your world? Try doing a rough back-of-the-envelope calculation as we've done here. Take the salaries and compensation of your salespeople and sales managers, add them together, and divide the total by the average number of sales calls made per year to reach an average cost per sales call. Take 60 percent of your answer, and that is the number of dollars being wasted per sales call. Imagine approaching an office coordinator in the exact same way that you approach a chief financial officer. The aggregate of wasted access is staggering. Unfortunately it is all too common.

So what's the difference between the strategic, high-level sale and the consultative sale to lower levels of management? We will shortly assert that, at its core, the business of business is the consummation of a *free-will* exchange for *mutual benefit*, initiated and facilitated by the salesperson. Three factors determine the level of an organization at which that exchange takes place:

- Time horizons
- Consequences
- Costs

The longer the time horizon, the more dramatic the consequences, the more expensive the proposition, and the higher in the organization the dialogue is likely to take place. It's not a static thing; as these factors grow longer, broader, and higher, they become the domain of more senior personnel.

Time Horizons

Technically, the phrase "time horizon" refers to the interval during which an investment program is to be completed. We have adapted it to refer to the investment of time, thought, and energy

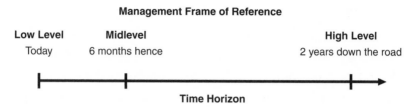

Figure 4.2

devoted to current and future events. Furthermore, we see it as an encompassing frame of reference—a vantage point from which to view the universe around you. There is quite a difference in the time horizon that serves as a frame of reference for the senior executive versus the lower-level manager (Figure 4.2). It is a matter of what one spends one's time thinking about, and really what one is paid to do.

Low-Level Management

Take, for example, an office coordinator as an average low-level manager. This person is typically paid to handle the mail, shipping and receiving, the procurement of office supplies, and so on. This is a person with a quintessentially short time horizon: it is today, and perhaps tomorrow, but seldom beyond that. This is because the kinds of things she deals with are principally problems, and she deals with those problems on an immediate basis. Packages must get out on time, mail must get sorted, and copier paper supply must be replenished. All of these are daily problems that must be attended to.

Midlevel Management

Now take a midlevel manager—the marketing director, for example. The marketing director oversees all marketing, advertising, and promotional staff and activities. He establishes marketing strategies to meet organizational objectives, and he is often responsible for some part in solving a strategic problem. It is his job to know who and how many prospects are in the pipeline, which is generally set at a 90- to 120-day horizon. It's also his job to keep the leads coming into the pipeline. He evaluates customer research, market conditions, and competitor data, and he implements marketing plan changes when necessary. The marketing director makes decisions with a much longer time horizon than the office coordinator, but these decisions still tend to be made only two or three months in advance—or in some cases six.

High-Level Management

Let's now reach higher up to executive management. In fact, let's imagine the CEO of a Fortune 1000 company. Her primary job is *not* to think about the problems the company is facing today. Instead, the CEO is paid primarily to think a year down the road; two years down the road; over the visible horizon. The board of directors, the investors, and the stockholders want to know how she is going to transform the company into a larger, more profitable company. What it isn't about is right now. The function of the CEO is to implement the strategic goals and objectives of the organization, to enable the board to fulfill its governance function, and to give direction and leadership toward the achievement of the organization's philosophy, mission, and strategy, and its annual goals and objectives. It's all rather lofty, but the key point is that each aspect of the CEO's function requires the ability to look over the horizon—to read trends, to prognosticate accurately and wisely. And as you can see in the graph in Figure 4.3, the CEO's frame of reference is a long time horizon.

Obviously, then, if you want to talk the language of executive management, you need to be looking at problems that may befall the unwary executive unexpectedly two years down the road and solutions to those problems that are unanticipated. Indeed, all four

Figure 4.3

Client Insight Creators, as we shall see, work perfectly for the senior executive because it's not about right now. It's about the future.

As you rise in the organization—that is to say, as you move up the corporate ladder in your selling endeavor—the problems you help the customers discover have to either become more broad in the sense that they concern the whole enterprise or become much longer in the sense that they are much further off in time. Or both. The office coordinator cares about the lost package, and that's all she cares about. The CEO cares about the overarching strategy of the company and its impact on the company's growth. Very different.

Consequences

"Consequences" refers to the repercussions that will befall our customer if his buying decision is a bad one; and the rewards that will be reaped if his decision leads to success. Both are a matter of degree.

Low-Level Management

We return to our plucky office coordinator and discover that if she makes a mistake, disaster does not ensue. The lights stay on, and the office does not come grinding to a halt. Let's say a package gets lost; another will be sent a day late. Or the printer runs out of paper. Most inconvenient. Irritating even. But not disastrous. Failure is not beset by huge consequences; and on the flip side, success is not attended by great rewards. In short, a "grave" mistake by the office coordinator is not devastating to the company— it is a small consequence. The office coordinator doesn't usually even show up on a P&L statement; she's absorbed in a larger budget. She has an impact only on the expense line, and not a significant impact at that.

Midlevel Management

If the marketing director makes a mistake, there is a larger consequence. It hurts. The doors won't close, but it could be a tough thing. Let's suppose a new direct-mail campaign fails. It could negatively affect the bottom line. It will certainly impact company revenue negatively. Failure at the level of the marketing director may not cripple a company, but it will surely matter more than mistakes made at lower levels of management.

High-Level Management

When the CEO makes a dramatic error or fails to be cognizant of something (makes a poor judgment or otherwise blunders), the whole company can go downhill. There are often dire consequences. A CEO's roll of the dice is usually for high stakes. One thinks of the eight-track tape, Sony's Betamax, or the American car companies' failure to join the fuel economy revolution. Conversely, if she gets it right, there are huge rewards. Consider Toyota's hybrid Prius or the Apple iPod. Everything comes up roses. If the CEO's purview were to shift dramatically up or down, we're talking about the whole profit of the entire company. That would be enormous: Either stockholders would be building an altar to her or she'd be looking for another job—and so would a lot of other people. The acid test is would it materially affect the operating capacity of the company. It's sort of a 1-to-10 scale: the closer to 10, the higher the consequence. The CEO affects all five of the business areas: revenue, cost of sales, margin, expenses, and profit. When selling to executive management, be keenly aware of the consequences that are being faced by those with serious decision-making authority. Never underestimate the power of the human mind to rationalize hard choices. The research shows that the seriousness of consequences at the high level will often be disguised by a laser-like focus on price (Figure 4.4).

Level of Management

Figure 4.4

Costs: Investment Required

The significance of the investment required lies in its relativity to other big-ticket items, profits, and revenue in the company. We use "costs" plural because opportunity costs are included in the reckoning. The larger the investment relative to the amount of revenue the company generates, or the profit it makes, the more involved the sale is. Costs are calculated on the basis of the size of the company. For Exxon-Mobil, $2½ million might be a rounding error, but for the $20 million company, it may be three-fourths of its profit (Figure 4.5).

Low-Level Management

When the office coordinator orders office supplies, she doesn't consult the CEO—or anyone else for that matter. Small-ticket items lie in the realm of the consultative seller. The Unrecognized Problem and the Unanticipated Solution play regularly at this level. In contrast, if the salesperson who comes in to see the office coordinator wants to talk about revenue and team morale, he's not going to make it.

Midlevel Management

The marketing director has a much larger budget than his lower-level colleagues, but he too is a terrific candidate for the consultative sale. The first two Client Insight Creators can play spectacularly well at this level. At midlevel management the time horizon has grown a bit longer, and/or the consequences have become a bit more

Figure 4.5

dramatic, and/or costs have become significantly elevated, beyond what a low-level manager would be allowed to decide upon. In short, it's beyond the pay grade of the low-level manager.

High-Level Management

If you're going to get the attention of executive management, either the cost has to be so significant that the CEO pays attention or the reward on the benefits side of the Value Equation (value = benefits – cost) has to be potentially enormous. If middle management wanted to spend $2½ million on new product development, the CEO of a $20 million company would no doubt be intimately involved in the decision. On the other hand, at a Fortune 100 company, $2½ million would get lost in the background noise, and it would be very difficult indeed to capture the interest of a CEO. You may be able to get the CEO's attention if you can do such good work with your $2½ million product or service that you can make the amplification of that relatively minor expense come out to a huge return on investment.

Just a quick note on the subject of opportunity costs: by spending significant money in one place (say, product development) as opposed to another (perhaps buying a company to expand presence in the Asia Pacific), the CEO of a company faces an opportunity cost as well as a real cost. By opting for one purchase over another, she is essentially losing out on an opportunity.

If the salesperson gets in to see the CEO but all the salesperson wants to talk about is some expense line, it had better be a giant part of expenses. For example, the CEO would listen to somebody who said, "I can cut your travel costs in half without affecting anyone's schedule." Well, that's someone she'd listen to. On the other hand, if a salesperson said, "I can cut your copy paper expenses in half," the CEO would show him the door and probably not even recommend that he talk to the office coordinator. So it's a magnitude

Figure 4.6

issue as well as a breadth issue: the more you narrow it down to a single category, the greater must be the magnitude of its impact (Figure 4.6).

Implications for Selling at the Executive Level

The first thing you should notice is that by selling at the executive level, you broaden the number of Client Insight Creators at your disposal precisely because they are focused on these different horizons. The reason that the opportunity for value creation opens so wide as you reach the executive level is that the horizons of what they care about are so broad, particularly the time horizons. By virtue of the fact that they have more latitude to make decisions, there is greater potential application of the Client Insight Creators. The authority as well as the responsibility to make decisions expands according to the three factors. As you move above the junior executive, the definitions of those five components of the financial statement where you focus have to be much broader.

Because of this broad decision-making authority and responsibility, the senior executive needs to know more and needs to have a greater breadth of understanding. And the larger the need for understanding, the greater the opportunity for the salesperson to provide value through the Client Insight Creators.

We must warn you that you will be tempted to think the Client Insight Creators are homogenous. Resist the temptation. They are not. The point of this chapter is to make it clear that there is a whole function that you need to be appreciative of and that you really ought to swim with the current. The current is that you need to create these environments in which you can make a free-will exchange of *mutual* benefit. And grasping that forces the question, If that means mutual benefit, where does one go to find these benefits that accrue to one's client? Well, you've got to look inside those five functions of the income statement, and you've got to take them apart—that's how you'll get there.

Having an understanding of the business of business is a prerequisite for selling to senior executives. It should be taught right out of college, but it rarely is. Most sellers never learn the fundamentals of commerce, and they can do fine. But they never achieve greatness. In truth your youthful days of selling were probably fairly tactical. But as you climb the ladder, it becomes ever more important to understand the context in which sales take place. As the consequences of your sales get larger, as the time horizon extends outward, as the amount of money involved increases, it becomes absolutely *de rigueur*.

So let's take a step back. Let's draw our attention for a moment to the broad question: What is the business of business? We need to explore this in some depth because a proper understanding of the fundamentals of commercial enterprise is crucial to value creation, especially at the strategic level. We've discussed the factors that define selling to the executive; let's now look at why it matters.

THE FUNDAMENTALS OF COMMERCIAL ENTERPRISE AND THE STRATEGIC SELLER

The business of business is the consummation of a *free-will* exchange for *mutual benefit*, initiated and facilitated by the salesperson. Although it's a relatively straightforward concept, it is rarely thought of in those terms. You used to be able to kind of fake your way through selling (or at the very least get away with inadequate skills) because the market lacked information. That is no longer true. Have you, the seller, ever stopped to consider what the actual business of business is? Because if you think it's about getting money for your products, you're wrong. It's about creating a space where there's this mutually beneficial exchange conducted at the free will of the customer.

The business of business has been since time immemorial about an exchange in which both parties are better off by virtue of the exchange (Figure 4.7). Sellers unfortunately oftentimes unconsciously think that one of the two parties to the exchange is going to lose. But commerce never works that way. Commerce—the trafficking of goods and services—is about both of us being

Figure 4.7

better off because of what we gave and what we got. From that principle then, the seller is at the very nexus of the exchange. And the job of the seller is to create the atmosphere in which the buyer can recognize the benefits of the exchange so that it can take place by the *free-will* choice of the buyer.

Products and services are no longer as diverse and different as they once were (in fact, they are more plentiful and more similar than they used to be), and they're widely *viewed* as commodities by the marketplace. There is a limited amount of time in which a product has a uniqueness phase. Consider the MP3 player or plasma TV (introduced to consumers by Pioneer in December 1997 and followed quickly by Panasonic); or the GPS system in your car; or smart phones; or Blue Ray versus HD Disc. By the time the market catches up to that uniqueness factor, imitators have arrived. So there's a general impression of commoditization. It isn't a purely commoditized world, but it might as well be from the seller's point of view. The seller is no longer getting rewarded for the differences. The only way to get rewarded for the differences is down the path of seller expertise—the medium of exchange by which the buyer benefits. The recognition of this simple truth separates the strategic seller from the throng of average sellers.

But let's return to the central issue, which is about the business of business and the facilitation of the exchange—the idea that the salesperson is at the very nexus of the business of business. It's the strategic salesperson that initiates and facilitates the free-will exchange. It will take place only if mutual benefit accrues to both parties. Too many salespeople don't seem to realize that. Too many salespeople seem to think of sales as a battleground that they must enter to get the most they can get. It is a battle that the buyer is going to fight and that someone is going to win. Even though we dress it up by saying we're "customer focused," a battleground is what many tend to imagine.

And all too often we think that sales is just about questions or models. It's not. It's about this atmosphere we must facilitate in which the opportunity for that *free-will* decision can flourish.

The principle of free will really is important. And it is frequently overlooked. Salespeople often think in terms of selling by an iron will (the *Glengarry Glen Ross* approach)—just keep on hammering until they buy. The buyers these days are rather free will oriented because they don't have to take your call anymore; they don't have to talk to you anymore; and they don't have to see you anymore. The iron will of the seller will never overcome the free will of the buyer. The seller must create the environment in which the buyer's free will is intact. There are, however, important exceptions.

For the sake of contrast, let's look at the rare moments when the free will of a buyer is not an option and where there is no free-will choice. Governments, for example, which protect the interests of their citizens, make certain things illegal and regulate others:

- Many drugs are proscribed because addiction robs one of free will. Drug addiction leaves the unfortunate addict with a nonoption as regards drugs. He must have the drug of choice or suffer.

- Monopolies are broken up or, in the case of public utilities, they are regulated. A monopoly forces a non-free-will exchange on the part of the buyer; she must pay the asking price (whether it is fair or not and whether she likes it or not) or go without. Government regulation therefore prevents all but a few monopolies, from operating, such as public utility companies, which are necessary to our well-being.

A few regulated monopolies make our lives better. Even though we have lost our free will, it's preferable that we be able to flip a switch and get power or turn on the tap and get pure drinking water. But here are two cases in which the loss of free will is deemed acceptable in the course of commerce: that which is illegal and that which is regulated for the good of the citizenry. As a general rule, the free will of the buyer—*in an atmosphere of mutually beneficial exchange created by the seller*—is paramount for the wheels of commerce to turn smoothly.

THE CHANGING LANDSCAPE OF BENEFITS

Up until recently, all of the benefit to a buyer accrued *after* he bought something. The revolution in sales is that that benefit must now move *prior* to the transaction. What's happened is that you have to be creating mutual benefit *in the exchange of time*. The person who's using these Client Insight Creators has to recognize you're try-ing to create a value, an atmosphere of mutually beneficial ex-change, *before* you ever sell anything. Today, a senior executive will not invest time without the promise of an immediate return on that investment. Patience is not considered a virtue. The benefits don't only accrue afterward but before. So what does that mean?

Our research at Huthwaite has revealed that there is a pre-dictable pattern to the way buyers make complex purchasing decisions. That pattern of behavior forms an excellent way of look-ing at how the benefits part of the exchange has migrated. Let's be-gin then with a description of that process and then show you against it how benefits have changed. The buying pattern normally progresses through four distinct stages. These stages are *recogni-tion of needs, evaluation of options, resolution of concerns*, and then, after the *decision* has been made and the purchase consum-mated, *implementation*. Following implementation is a period of *changes over time* that begin the cycle anew. This is graphically represented in Figure 4.8.

The Customer Decision-Making Process

Figure 4.8

In the recognition of needs stage, the customer is becoming aware of a problem that needs to be solved. When the problem becomes sufficiently acute, and the decision to take action has been made, the customer moves into evaluation of options. In this stage the customer is looking for possible solutions to the problem and assessing choices. Once an option has been chosen, the customer generally moves into a period of subtle anxiety (resolution of concerns) stemming from a fear of the consequences of making a wrong decision. If these fears are satisfactorily allayed, the decision is made to buy. Following the purchase there's usually a stage of implementation during which the seller continues to support and help the account.

As you can see in Figure 4.9, benefits that had previously been enjoyed by the buyer only after the sales transaction are now expected to be part of the sales process itself (that is, there is an expectation that benefits to the buyer will accrue *prior* to the actual purchase of goods and services). When value was embodied in the product or service, the benefit was by definition going to

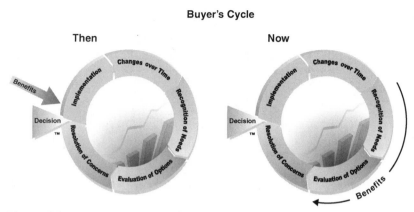

Figure 4.9

accrue to the buyer after the purchase. Since products and services have begun to be viewed by the buying community as commoditized, the only way to be differentiated on anything but price is to accrue benefits before the purchase. It is a great challenge. But it is very doable. We shall look at the tactics of moving the benefits forward in the sales process in the ensuing chapters. It does not mean that the sales cycle must get longer. It does mean that you have to provide benefits that are not directly related to the product or service you are selling.

The question is, how do you contextualize your job in the idea that you must create the atmosphere in which mutually beneficial exchange takes place? The sales process is really about crafting an environment in which both parties are well served. But remember, because the buyer controls the relationship, she must be well served *first*!

The insurance industry provides an excellent example of how this works. Indeed, the insurance industry has been dealing with exactly this problem for some 50 years or more. For one thing, people outside the insurance business don't generally really understand insurance. Most people have never even read their insurance policies; they are inscrutable to the untrained eye. For another thing, insurance policies are widely viewed as a nuisance at best, a necessary evil at worst. There is consequently a strong tendency for people to buy insurance on price alone (a good example is Geico: "15 minutes could save you 15 percent or more"). Move from the consumer to the business context, and it's no different.

The sellers in the insurance business have therefore had to take one of two approaches: either they decide to be the cheap one (and grind on their risk assessors to try and give you the lowest bid), or they decide to provide service before they sell a policy, preferably in the form of making the client a better or more successful business. Great insurance salespeople have thus for years been providing auxiliary services. For a long time there have been many unrecognized problems relative to workplace safety. Especially now with OSHA regulatory oversight, such problems are even more significant. Risk assessors study these workplace safety issues in their minutiae.

The good insurance salesperson doesn't go in to a company and say, "I'll give it to you for a lower rate." Instead, he says, "I'll reduce your risk. And if I reduce your risk, your incidence of accidents will go down, and the cost of your property and casualty insurance will become more stable." The salesperson reduces risk by identifying unrecognized work safety problems.

There was a day and age when property and casualty insurance was provided by only a few companies, and it was such a low-level cost that it was an immaterial budget item. Its cost began to rise dramatically as lawsuits began to produce a tremendous number of settlements. And as more and more regulation was passed and more and more lawsuits were waged, the cost went up literally a hundredfold. Well, now this type of insurance is a big deal. Today you probably don't sell business insurance without talking to a very senior executive. And that very senior executive is paying attention because the insurance purchase has consequences; he cannot be underinsured, and the insurance costs a tremendous amount of money. Insurance salespeople now have the attention of a very senior executive, who wants to make that cost as low as possible. So if you don't provide some other services such as workplace safety evaluations, you're not in the game unless you're the lowest-cost provider. In short, the buyer in the insurance industry has been accruing benefits *prior* to the actual purchase of insurance for years. The rest of the world is catching on.

Business, as we have said, is—at its most fundamental core—the exchange between buyer and seller for mutual benefit. Both emerge from the exchange better off; otherwise, it's not business.

That's also what being *customer focused* is: it's not asking a specific type of question per se; it's understanding that you have this desire to establish a mutually beneficial exchange—and you are willing to invest before the sale to make that happen. When you do that well, you carve it out in such a way that you're the only one who can make that exchange.

Let's think about how those benefits look from the perspective of the person who's going to control that exchange, the buyer. It's no longer possible to have your benefits be unique such that you are the only seller who can offer them. It has to be the way it's sold. Therefore, by definition "value" has now migrated from what you sold—the after-the-transaction benefit—to what has to occur (at least, a lot of it) before the sale is concluded.

When you are dealing with the strategic part of selling, as depicted in Figure 4.10—that is, the Unseen Opportunity and the Broker of Strengths—the first thing you have to understand is the frame of reference. And that frame of reference begins with a fundamental understanding of what business is about. While this is actually true of all the Client Insight Creators, it is particularly important when working at the senior executive level. Keep the business of business running through your mind as you read the

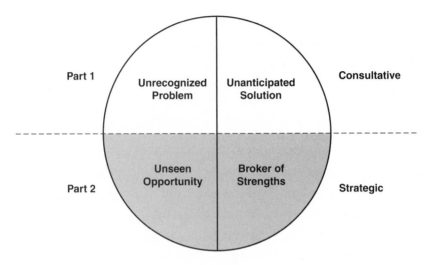

Figure 4.10

next chapters on the strategic Client Insight Creators, the Unseen Opportunity and the Broker of Strengths.

To summarize, the successful strategic seller must focus on three major themes when selling at the executive management level:

1. Three factors drive the elevation of a purchasing decision within an organization: time horizons, consequences, and investment required (costs).

2. The "business of business" means that buyer and seller make an exchange for *mutual benefit*. The strategic salesperson initiates and facilitates that *free-will* exchange.

3. Senior executives go through predictable phases when making a purchasing decision, and benefits must accrue throughout the decision-making process, not just after the transaction has been completed.

We're going to take one step further now and discuss how to create value at the executive level. Only a rare few sellers understand how to sell strategically, and therefore, only a rare few are successful at the executive level. Chapter 5 focuses on the strategic seller and the third Client Insight Creator, the Unseen Opportunity.

KEY POINTS

☞ The Unseen Opportunity and the Broker of Strengths play largely at the strategic, or executive, level.

☞ We define "strategic sales" as high-level selling; either as selling to executive management or enterprise-to-enterprise selling. "Consultative selling," while it can take place at every echelon of a corporation, cannot take place with every customer.

☞ Three factors determine the level of an organization at which a free-will exchange for mutual benefit, initiated and facilitated by the salesperson (the definition of the "business of business"), takes place:

1. *Time horizons.* The investment of time, thought, and energy devoted to current and future events. The further into the future the effect occurs, the higher in the organization the decision will be made.

2. *Consequences.* The repercussions that will befall our customer if his buying decision is a bad one and the rewards that will be reaped if the decision leads to success. Both are a matter of degree. The greater the repercussions or rewards, the higher in the organization the decision will be made.

3. *Costs.* The significance of the investment required lies in its relativity to other big-ticket items, profits, and revenue in the company. The greater the costs, the higher in the organization the decision will be made.

☞ By selling at the executive level, the seller broadens the number of Client Insight Creators at his or her disposal

precisely because executives are focused on longer time
horizons, larger consequences, and higher costs.

☞ From the perspective of the salesperson, the *business of
business* is the consummation of a free-will exchange
for mutual benefit, initiated and facilitated by the
salesperson.

☞ A fundamental shift in sales has come to pass because
many of the benefits to the buyer must now occur *prior* to
the transaction's conclusion.

☞ Customers go through a predictable set of stages in the
decision-making process:

1.   Recognition of needs
2.   Evaluation of options
3.   Resolution of concerns
4.   (Decision)
5.   Implementation
6.   Changes over time

and their perspective on value alters as they move through
these stages.

Unrecognized Problem	Unanticipated Solution
Unseen Opportunity	Broker of Strengths

EXPLORING THE UNSEEN OPPORTUNITY

> Opportunity is missed by most because it is dressed in overalls and looks like work.
>
> —Thomas A. Edison

HELP them imagine opportunities that they would not otherwise explore.

Let us look one last time at pattern recognition, that peculiar brilliance that informs knowledge, and let us remember that pattern recognition is an acquired skill.

What do you see in the image in Figure 5.1? What if we were to ask if you see any sort of bovine features: large, sad eyes; a long face? Could it be a portrait of a cow? Ah, now you see it. So it is with the Unseen Opportunity. It may be right in front of you—and obvious once you see it—but the pattern does not emerge until the right questions are asked.

Business executives are paid to produce the outcome that is *desirable but not inevitable*. Let that sink in a moment. Indeed, it bears repeating: *Business executives are paid to produce the outcome that is desirable but not inevitable.* And that doesn't always mean solving problems. As a matter of fact, solving problems no longer serves.

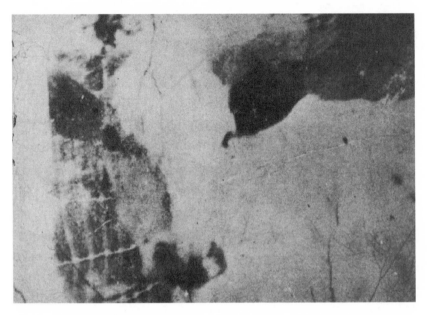

Figure 5.1
Source: Karl Dallenbach, "A Puzzle-Picture with a New Principle of Concealment." From *American Journal of Psychology.* Copyright 1951 by the Board of Trustees of the University of Illinois. Used with permission of the University of Illinois Press.

In the 1970s and 1980s, executives were paid to solve problems. They're not anymore. Other people solve problems. They're now paid to create opportunities. When we say "create opportunities," we mean create new and additional business—in other words, profit that is greater than the acceptable level that they have established or that has been established for them by a board of directors.

DEFINITION OF THE UNSEEN OPPORTUNITY

As the Unanticipated Solution is about helping a client to redefine the connection between the problem and the outcome (or redefine the outcome), the Unseen Opportunity is about helping a client redefine *desirable but not inevitable*. As we move through the continuum of problem to solution to outcome, we meet the opportunity at the outcome. But it's more than the outcome the client has defined as desirable; it's over and above; it's a new definition of "desirable" based on the art of the possible. The Unseen Opportunity produces an aha moment that sounds something like "Gosh, it never would have occurred to me that such a thing is even theoretically possible!"

The Unseen Opportunity differs from the Unanticipated Solution especially thus: you do not begin with a problem that needs to be solved (Figure 5.2). Both the Unrecognized Problem and the Unanticipated Solution begin in the context of a problem; one unknown to the customer (but known to you) and the other well known to the customer (but to which you have a better solution than the customer has mapped out, or a better outcome). With the Unseen Opportunity there is no particular problem with the way the customer is doing business, but there is an absence of maximum outcome.

You can think about it from the standpoint of the application of the customer's capabilities and assets to markets in which she is not currently playing. What problems can the customer solve that she

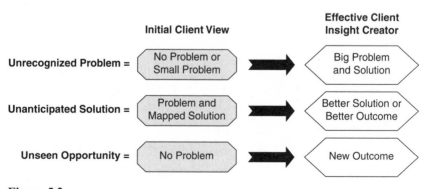

Figure 5.2

is not currently leveraging? What new outcomes can she produce for her existing customers; and what outcomes can she produce in a totally untapped market?

Remember the exercises you went through when considering the Unrecognized Problem and the Unanticipated Solution? You sought problems in your customer's industry that he might be unaware of and that you could solve, and you looked at optimal solutions to problems about which your customer was painfully aware. Now we are essentially asking you to do the same thing in the context of your customer's customer. What problems can your customer solve for his customer that he is not doing? What optimal solutions does your customer have for his customer's problems that he is not addressing?

Value creation using the Unseen Opportunity occurs *de novo*. It's a recognition issue. It's recognition that there is more out there to be gained than is currently being wrung from the marketplace. It's really about opening the eyes of your customer to an opportunity he has that he doesn't see, which importantly is *not* going to bring the business down if it is not exercised as an option. That really is an important point: failing to exploit the opportunity will *not* negatively impact the business.

One thinks of the man who sold engine oil to UPS. One day it occurred to him that UPS was pretty good at fleet maintenance; and what's more, operations research appeared to be the company's forte because it was handling fleet logistics with aplomb. He suggested that UPS consider getting into the logistics and fleet maintenance consulting business. So it did. And a multimillion-dollar consulting business was born at UPS. His observation was revolutionary; but note that absent the revelation, UPS was doing just fine. It was above and beyond its current revenue stream. It was a matter of opening management's eyes to their own capabilities and applying their assets and capabilities to a new market. Value

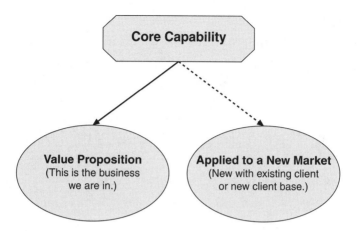

Figure 5.3

creation occurs here when you discover the intersection of your own capability with the customer's untapped capability.

As depicted in Figure 5.3, your customer has a core capability to sell. The sale of that core capability is the customer's value proposition; it is the business the company is in. The opportunity unseen by your customer is how that core capability might be applied to a new market within the company's existing client base, or a new client base altogether.

Occasionally you will present an Unseen Opportunity to a client or customer in what may appear to be an altruistic way. That is to say, the opportunity you bring forward may have no direct bearing on the growth of your own business within the client company. But it is never purely altruistic as you are always generating value for the client.

That said, in an ideal world you are seeking to help the customer exploit opportunities that will impact your own business; that will expand your own presence within your customer's business. You are trying to work out what outside force in the world might generate more sales for your customer that will pull through more business for yourself. If your client sells services, the way to affect your own bottom line is by helping him to expand his business either by headcount or by physical assets. You are looking for expansion of the business that is acceleration beyond the organic.

CREATING THE UNSEEN OPPORTUNITY

Let's now return to the Business Impact (Value) Zone—the inter-section of questioning skills, business acumen, and industry knowledge (Figure 5.4). And let's work out how each of these

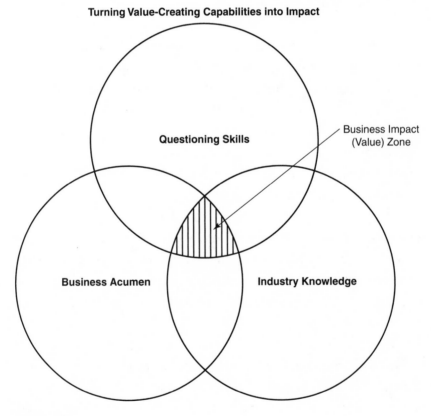

Turning Value-Creating Capabilities into Impact

Questioning Skills

Business Impact (Value) Zone

Business Acumen

Industry Knowledge

Figure 5.4

plays in the strategic development of the Unseen Opportunity. Again, we must emphasize that the Unseen Opportunity is generally offered at mid- to upper-level management and in the C suite. It is still a matter of pattern recognition, and the divulgence of the pattern is still accomplished through questioning, not telling. Questioning skill again plays a major role—as does business acumen. You have to have a really solid foundational understanding of the basic principles of business in order to recognize potential opportunities for your customers. Industry knowledge in this case is of a general kind, but it is no less important. It is again at the intersection of these three that value comes alive for the customer.

Questioning Skills

Again we return to the Boundary Conditions of Human Communication, and specifically to the first Confirmation Bias: people value what *they say* and their own conclusions more than what *they are told.* The skill at work in this case is the ability to help the client make discoveries through knowledgeable questioning. The particular discoveries we are concerned with are (1) a new opportunity with existing customers and/or (2) an opportunity to serve a new client base with unutilized or underleveraged company capabilities. We are questioning with a view to opening the eyes of the customer such that she will see her company's own capabilities in a new light. We are guiding her to certain conclusions. We are helping her to figure out what her company does better than everyone else in its marketspace. And then we are leading her to discover how she can best take advantage of these capabilities and optimize the opportunity now revealed to her.

Business Acumen

As with the Unanticipated Solution, it pays to understand the fundamentals of commercial enterprise when dealing with the Unseen Opportunity. It behooves the salesperson to understand *a priori* the potentialities intrinsic to his customer's business. It is important to understand how certain capabilities can create an outcome that affects one or more of the five business fundamentals discussed in the last chapter. Know your customer's business intimately. It may be important to understand your customer's company strategy so that you can eventually map your own products or services to his desired business outcomes. More to the point, however, you want your customer to realize that you know his business. It establishes trust. Remember, you are most likely dealing with the C suite, or close to it. The acid test for the Unseen Opportunity is this: What does your client do that's auxiliary to the company's main business that would not improve its quality by outsourcing? In other words, what does your client do so well that outside assistance would be of no benefit to him? These are core capabilities that could be used on something other than the client's traditional value proposition. Herein lies opportunity.

Industry Knowledge

Broad, if general, industry knowledge is a prerequisite for effective exploration of the Unseen Opportunity. You want to be able to see across a very wide horizon. Recall the salesman we mentioned earlier who sold oil to UPS. His observation that UPS was doing (and still does) a marvelous job of vehicle maintenance and fleet management required a general knowledge of the competitive landscape. Remember, the man just sold engine oil (and now sells a lot more of it to UPS customers!), but he kept his eyes wide open.

SKILLS IN ACTION: HOW IT'S DONE

A classic Unseen Opportunity was recently described to us by our friend Tim McManus, administrator and chief operating officer at Trinity Medical Center in Birmingham, Alabama. Trinity had recently sent out a request for proposal for environmental services (that is, housekeeping) at the hospital. Tim explained to us that a housekeeper in a hospital plays a vitally important role because the whole hospital is essentially the front office—it gives the first impression. Unlike janitorial services in an industrial complex or an office building, hospital housekeepers have to clean up around occupants. That is to say, patients see housekeepers almost as often as they see nurses!

Environmental services, it must be said, is a pure commodity. Almost all providers use the same basic cleaning agents and chemicals; and just about anyone can be trained to clean properly. So how do you differentiate among companies that at first glance all look exactly the same? We asked Tim why he chose Professional Services—which was neither the largest company, nor the cheapest—for the contract award. His answer was fascinating. He said that Professional Services had talked about cultural mesh; it described its housekeepers as being integral parts of the healthcare experience. In other words, Professional Services was offering far more than housekeeping; it was offering professional employees who see themselves in a sense as health-care professionals. Since housekeepers are provided 24 hours a day, seven days a week, Professional Services was offering the Unseen Opportunity to add 100 staff of second-line care for the hospital's patients.

You may be wondering why this is regarded as an Unseen Opportunity rather than an Unanticipated Solution. It is true that Trinity had a need and had mapped a path to a solution (that is,

Trinity had a need for best-in-class environmental services, and it had shopped the need to four potential vendors), giving this the appearance of an Unanticipated Solution. And it would have been classed as one had Professional Services talked only of the cultural mesh that provides a better outcome. Professional Services went much further, however, and offered not only the Unanticipated Solution of 100 exceptional housekeepers who would mesh culturally with the hospital but also the Unseen Opportunity to add 100 new staff of second-line health-care providers *at no extra cost* to the hospital.

We called Ira Levy, president and CEO of Professional Services, to get his take on the partnership. Not surprisingly, he talked about his company's motto of "Making a Difference"—not only for its clients but also for its employees. Environmental services employees tend to be less educated and tend to think of themselves as being on the bottom rung of the social ladder. Ira gives them dignity and professionalism; he has built a culture based on "Recognition, Celebration, and Training." He teaches his people that they are a valuable and meaningful part of the overall health-care experience—a genuine part of the delivery of health-care services. He emphasizes kindness and caring and unprecedented acts of service excellence; and he then celebrates and rewards such behavior. Because his program is so enriching, he can field a force of excellent long-term employees.

"What we offered Trinity is a dedicated and professional environmental services force that performs their duties exceptionally well; but beyond that, they care for the patients. Anybody can be technically proficient in this job; our people really see themselves as part of the health-care process," said Ira.

In short, beyond mere exceptional housekeeping, Trinity in effect gets a completely unforeseen second-line of caring people to surround its patients with.

From Concept to Reality

Where does the Unseen Opportunity come from? How does it arise? Before we go any further, however, let us make one point very clear: the Unseen Opportunity is rarely the domain of the individual seller. Do not be disappointed if you (as an individual seller) *never* find one. You may come across a genuine opportunity to expand your customer's business (and your own, as a result) only once or twice in a lifetime. And if you do, be very grateful. Be always cognizant of what's going on at the intersection of your own business acumen and industry knowledge, and be ready to leap when an Unseen Opportunity does arise. But understand that it is not simple, and it is not something you can just decide to do. But keep a clear and open mind, just in case.

Now let us consider the exploration of the Unseen Opportunity at the strategic level. Begin by looking at the core capability (the hedgehog, if you remember Jim Collins's outstanding *Good to Great: Why Some Companies Make the Leap . . . and Others Don't* [Harper Collins, 2001]) that drives your customer's business. What are the enabling competencies that make it possible? What does your customer have to be really good at in order to make his business work successfully? Now reflect on how these enabling competencies might be used effectively in a new market space. In Figure 5.5, you will see what we're talking about. Each of the enabling capabilities feeds the core capability, which is the company's current value proposition. Someone arrives to reveal an Unseen Opportunity, and it becomes clear that these enabling capabilities might create a new market. The vertical dashed line represents the moment of discovery, when the realization is made that these ancillary capabilities may in fact be turned outward and become core capabilities themselves in a new market.

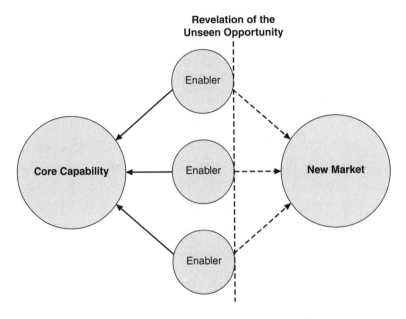

Figure 5.5

Let's look at an example of what we're talking about. Consider NASCAR pit crews. Winning a NASCAR race often depends on shaving literally *thousandths* of a second off of time in the pit. The average NASCAR pit stop lasts between 13 and 14 seconds. It includes four fresh 65-pound tires, 22 gallons of fuel (each gravity-driven 11-gallon fuel can—which weighs over 80 pounds—will empty its contents in about 5.7 seconds), a clean windshield, and water for the driver—in less than 14 seconds. NASCAR races are literally won or lost in the pit.

Pit crews depend on teamwork, lightning speed, and efficiency to a degree that boggles the mind. There may be no greater example of the combination of speed and team choreography anywhere in the sports world, or in any field of human endeavor for that matter. Their core capability is the ability to get a race car in and out of the pit in seconds—fully prepared for the next laps of the race. The chief enabling competencies are teamwork, speed, and efficiency. As it turns out, these and other special enabling competencies such as preparedness and safety have tremendous market value in and of themselves.

In July 2000, Breon M. Klopp founded 5 OFF 5 ON Race Team Performance to provide a specific and marketable set of skills as over-the-wall pit crew members to people that desired a career in motorsports. It was the first school of its kind. Prior to that time, pit crews trained their own or poached members from other established teams. In April 2003, PIT Instruction and Training, LLC, purchased 5 OFF 5 ON Race Team Performance to better meet the increasing demands of the sport. PIT, incidentally, is owned by Tom DeLoach (former CFO of Mobil Corporation). DeLoach began to explore a previously Unseen Opportunity. He recognized that the auxiliary skills required for effective pit crews might be analogous to the skills needed in the corporate world, especially agile manufacturing.

In 2006, United Airlines sent 1,200 supervisory "lead" ramp workers to "PIT Crew U," a program of PIT Instruction and Training in Mooresville, North Carolina. While not intending to turn airport runways into race tracks, United did hope to shave eight minutes off of the average aircraft ground time. Having just come off of three years of bankruptcy protection, it was in no position to buy new jetliners. But it reckoned it could add more than 100 flights per *day* by saving the extra time on the ground. It has so far proved very effective. PIT is working with United Airlines and other companies to promote safety, efficiency, preparation, and communication to increase productivity in manufacturing and service industries (Figure 5.6).

Breon M. Klopp, senior director of motorsports development, PIT Instruction and Training, said:

> What we've done is use something very basic, which is the concept of a pit crew, which most people are at least somewhat familiar with. We put our employees in a learning facility where

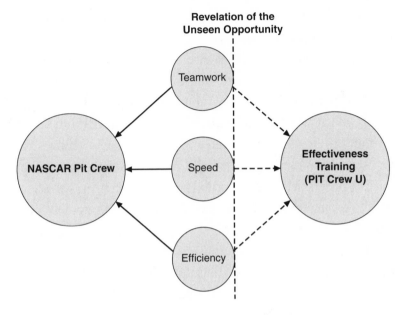

Figure 5.6

we apply situations that might occur in any workstation or any facility. We've broken it down to its lowest level, the smallest levels, and we've found that people are given something that they can take home and that they can immediately remember those three or five really key points. So they can go back to the facility and start implementing these points immediately, and they have a lot of enthusiasm because of the experience that they have.

PIT Crew U was not unfamiliar to the corporate world and it had done some training, but United really put it on the map as trainers *extraordinaire.*

From Concept to Reality, Continued

Now you must think through the consequences to the client of failing to react, or being unprepared to act, when the opportunity presents itself. Just think of the opportunity costs quite literally.

Preparation is the key to exploiting opportunities. Recall Louis Pasteur's observation back in 1854: "Chance favors only the prepared mind." What then are the consequences of an unprepared mind and, by extension, organization? What is likely to happen if your customer misses the proverbial boat? In the Trinity Medical Center case, it would be business as usual. By offering a whole new second line of patient care, Professional Services was literally able to recalibrate the definition of excellence. It provided the Unseen Opportunity to redefine *desirable but not inevitable.*

SKILLS IN ACTION: SELLING THE UNSEEN OPPORTUNITY

As you read through this next story, see if you can work out how the salespeople involved brought exceptional value in the form of an Unseen Opportunity to their respective customers.

Océ

A salesman for Océ (a Japanese manufacturer that produces high-end copy machines) went into a company that already had eight $100,000 copy machines. The company didn't need any more. But the technology it was using was dated, and it would have benefited to some degree by an upgrade to a new cadre of machines. The problem was that there was no money to pay for the upgrade, and the financial benefit wasn't worth the exchange. In other words, the benefits that would accrue to the client from getting the new technology were not outweighed by the hassle and the cost of the upgrade.

The Océ salesman contacted his company's finance department and worked out an arrangement whereby the financial people at Océ did a *purchase with a lease-back option.* This type of transaction is common in real estate, but it is not particularly common in the world of copy machines. By Océ's purchasing the equipment and then leasing it back to the customer, Océ's finance department was able to arrange for the incremental cost of the new machines to be so few pennies that the benefits accrued would then far outweigh the cost. Upgrading became an excellent value proposition, and the sale was made. That's another excellent example of the Unseen Opportunity. The client never had any idea that Océ had a finance capacity.

The Unseen Opportunity for Océ's client came in the form of a creative financing option that was utterly unexpected by the client. The Océ salesperson was able to work with his finance department to develop a plan that would allow the client to get the use of world-class copiers for a small monthly fee. The salesperson had helped the client redefine the *desirable but not inevitable* outcome (Figure 5.7).

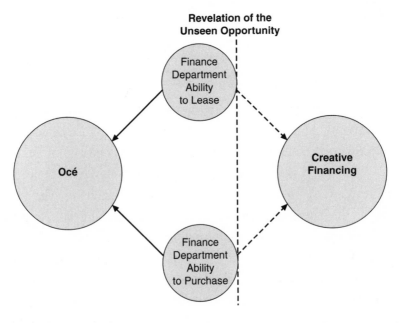

Figure 5.7

AND FINALLY

It is again time to return to your customers to find out when they have bought based on value rather than price and more to the point, when they have bought because an opportunity was revealed to them. By the way, there is no need for multiple trips to each of your customers to ask these specifics. Instead, design a survey that covers the field of the value propositions that have won the day. You can use this survey to gather the information you need to have to build an *arsenal of value.*

This project is something that you have to think through from a corporate perspective before you rush out and try to do it. The first step is to organize your list of customers into categories (who was transactional and who wasn't?). You can then examine the list to see where the areas are in which you can create value.

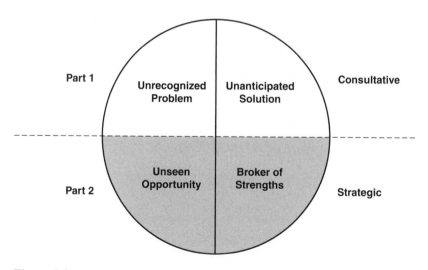

Figure 5.8

KEY POINTS

☞ *Definition of the "Unseen Opportunity."* The Unseen Opportunity is about helping the client redefine *desirable but not inevitable* outcomes. Take a core capability and apply it to a new market or a new client base altogether.

☞ Business executives are paid to produce the outcome that is desirable but not inevitable.

☞ The Business Impact (Value) Zone lies at the intersection of the following:

- *The seller's business acumen.* The salesperson needs to understand *a priori* the potentialities intrinsic to his customer's business. It is important to understand how certain capabilities can create an outcome that affects one or more of the five business fundamentals discussed in the last chapter.

- *The seller's industry knowledge.* The seller needs to be able to see across a very wide horizon, comparing his customer to the industry at large.

- *The seller's questioning skills.* Questioning skills need to be ever sharper and more sophisticated as the seller rises higher in the customer's organization.

☞ The Unseen Opportunity is generally offered at upper levels of management and/or at the C suite level of an organization.

☞ The Unseen Opportunity is rarely the domain of the individual seller.

| Unrecognized Problem | Unanticipated Solution |
| Unseen Opportunity | Broker of Strengths |

BROKER OF STRENGTHS: CROSS-SELLING

The only real voyage of discovery consists not in seeking new landscapes but in having new eyes.

—MARCEL PROUST

MAKE available to the customer the full capabilities of the seller's organization.

The first thing we need to understand about "brokering strengths" (or "brokering capabilities"—we shall use the terms interchangeably) is that it is impossible to do *de novo*. You have to have an existing relationship with the customer. We are talking about trying to embody a higher level of relationship. The second thing that's important to realize is that brokering strengths is actually cross-selling at the strategic level. We will discover that the Broker of Strengths is really a symbiosis of the other three Client Insight Creators.

THE SECRET TO CROSS-SELLING

Recall for a moment the description of the Broker of Strengths from Chapter 1. The seller serves as more than just a vendor of products and services but instead serves as a Broker of Strengths. Specifically, the seller serves to make available to the buyer the full range of capabilities of the seller's organization in such a way that these capabilities contribute to an expansion or redefinition of the customer's success. That is to say, the individual Broker of Strengths is the seller who can bring to bear the full array of his company's resources on behalf of the buyer to produce for the buyer a more desirable outcome.

We shall use the term "broker" in the sense of an intermediary or a middleman, and especially one who is able to set aside self-interest for the sake of the larger good. Done properly, brokering strengths produces a beneficial outcome for all involved in a transaction. Moreover, it is more powerful as a relationship solidifier than holding hands and singing Kumbaya. As we described in Chapter 6, the seller ought to be facilitating an exchange of *mutual benefit* wherein the buyer can make the *free-will decision* to buy. In this case the seller acts as an intermediary between the customer and his own company. The term used to define this capability is "cross-selling."

Cross-selling is potentially a powerful weapon in the arsenal of corporate America, and it has become a necessary one—because the competition is almost certainly trying it out to expand its market share. Brokering strengths used to be a "nice to have," but increasingly, due to certain trends in the marketplace we shall look at momentarily, it is becoming more and more compulsory.

TRENDS

There are several trends that are energizing cross-selling initiatives across most industries (Figure 6.1): *consolidation of suppliers* (tremendous merger and acquisition activity across the board has opened huge new markets within individual companies,

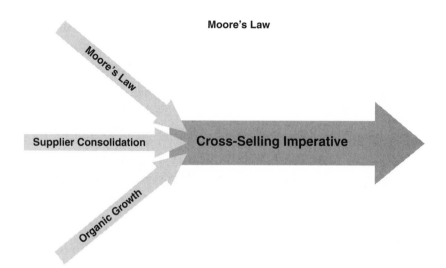

Figure 6.1

especially banks); *Moore's Law* (the exponential growth in product development means that companies are massively increasing their product offerings); and *organic growth* (business leaders are pushing hard for internal growth, which necessitates the expansion of existing relationships).

Consolidation of Suppliers

The first and most important driving force of cross-selling has emanated from the fact that every industry has followed the same accelerating trajectory: an ongoing consolidation of suppliers. The consolidation of corporate America is not unlike the Cold War arms race—it grows and accelerates in response to the competition. Thank goodness corporations do not have a policy of mutually assured destruction (MAD)! Think of IBM, Microsoft, and Google swallowing up companies wholesale. The data in Figure 6.2 show this consolidation. We shall be focusing particularly on banks, but you'll see that it is happening in every major industry.

As Kenneth Jones and Tim Critchfield pointed out in their fascinating article "Consolidation in the U.S. Banking Industry: Is the Long, Strange Trip About to End?"(*FDIC Banking Review*, vol. 17, no. 4, 2005):

> Over the two decades 1984–2003, the structure of the U.S. banking industry indeed underwent an almost unprecedented transformation—one marked by a substantial decline in the number of commercial banks and savings institutions and by a growing concentration of industry assets among a few dozen extremely large financial institutions.

As you can see in the graph in Figure 6.2, from the Jones and Critchfield article, there was tremendous consolidation in the U.S. banking industry in the almost 20 years between 1984 and 2003.

Number of Banking Organizations, 1984-2003

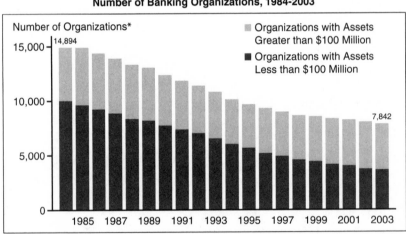

* Count is year-end includes only organizations that filed a financial report in the fourth quarter.

Figure 6.2

Source: Federal Deposit Insurance Corporation (FDIC), Kenneth D. Jones and Tim Critchfield, "Consolidation in the U.S. Banking Industry: Is the 'Long, Strange Trip' About to End?" *FDIC Banking Review*, vol. 17, no. 4, 2005. Permission granted.

Not only was there an almost 50 percent decrease in the overall number of banking organizations, but more significantly, organizations with assets greater than $100 million grew as a percentage of total banking organizations from about one-third to a little more than one-half.

Consider also these recent headlines:

The proposed merger of Bank of New York and Mellon Financial, announced in December, was greeted with fanfare as investors and analysts alike acclaimed the new group's standing as the world's biggest global custodian. The company, to be called Bank of New York Mellon, will have more than USD 16,600bn of assets under custody.—Rebecca Knight, "Birth of a Financial Powerhouse," *Financial Times*, London, February 13, 2007.

Wells Fargo's shares have been impressively consistent in beating those of peers, pretty much ever since the old bank was in effect taken over by Norwest in 1998. There are many good reasons for this. For one thing, the new bank had an early edge in cross-selling and never lost its touch at getting existing customers to buy ever more of its products. That says a lot about its ability to implement sensible ideas.— "Nimble Wells Fargo," *Financial Times*, London, January 7, 2007.

And it is happening in almost every major industry. In the graph in Figure 6.3 you can see the mergers and acquisitions (M&A) trend just for 1999, which was both a banner year and in many ways a typical year for the trend toward consolidation. Telecommunications tops the list with a staggering $172 billion in M&A deals *in just one year*. Banking, which is the archetypal industry for consolidation and consequent cross-selling, was tied for fourth, with $59 billion in M&A activity.

In the graph in Figure 6.4 you can see the difference in market share of the top five companies (in five different industries) between 1988 and 1998. You will note that the top five commercial

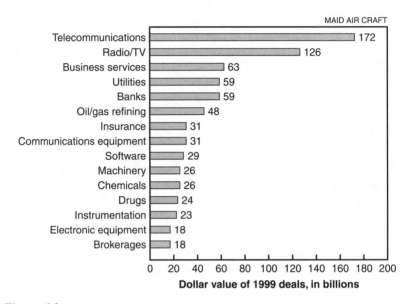

Figure 6.3

Source: Thomas Financial Securities Data (Mulligan, 1999). In Laura Baldwin, Frank Camm, and Nancy Moore, "Federal Contract Bundling: A Framework for Making and Justifying Decisions for Purchased Services," produced by and courtesy of the RAND Corporation.

banks in 1988 owned only 20 percent of market share. In 10 years, that more than doubled to 45 percent.

So why is there this trend toward consolidation? There are two major reasons: (1) to gain economies of scale, and (2) to create a market presence. In the case of banks, they want to expand their footprint. Over the past 20 or 30 years since the early eighties, banks have been allowed to get into a throng of new markets. Deregulation to allow banks to be more responsive to the marketplace has driven consolidation. A classic example is the huge number of interstate mergers that happened following passage of the Riegle-Neal Interstate Banking and Branching Efficiency Act of 1994.

And so with all this consolidation has come a spate of cross-selling initiatives and activities. As companies merge, they find they have customers who do not enjoy all the benefits of their new offerings.

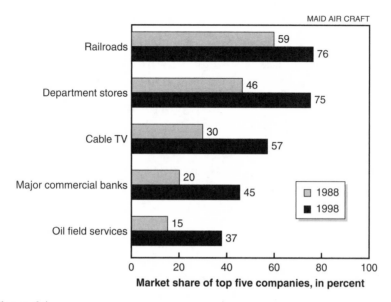

Figure 6.4

Note: Market share data reflect North American market except in case of oil field services, which is global.

Source: Thomas Financial Securities Data (Mulligan, 1999). In Laura Baldwin, Frank Camm, and Nancy Moore, "Federal Contract Bundling: A Framework for Making and Justifying Decisions for Purchased Services," produced by and courtesy of the RAND Corporation.

Extrapolation of Moore's Law

The second important factor in the increase in cross-selling initiatives is the exponential surge in product development and expansion across industries. This phenomenon is an extrapolation of Moore's Law. In 1965, Gordon Moore, director of the Research and Development Laboratories of the Fairchild Semiconductor Division of Fairchild Camera and Instrument Corp., observed that the number of transistors on an integrated circuit doubles every two years (a figure later updated to every 18 months). While Moore was looking at the empirical reality of transistor technology, the law does have a wider applicability. That is to say, the surge in product development and expansion across industries has been exponential. If not actually doubling every two years or 18 months, everything from crop development and new drugs to plasma television and SAP integration techniques seems to be improving and increasing at a very rapid pace. This means that most industries have more and better products to offer all the time. As companies increase their product offerings, cross-selling becomes absolutely necessary to survival against the competition that is already or soon afterward flogging the same improvements. There's just more stuff available.

The speed with which most industries seem to be developing is astonishing. And it is accelerating. Take the biotech industry as an example:

> The cost of sequencing live DNA into strings of nucleotide data falls dramatically every year, to the point where a single lab—Celera—has been able to challenge a multinational consortium of government labs in a race to sequence the human genome, simply by investing in next-generation sequencing equipment.—Clay Shirky, "Biotech's Version of Moore's Law," www.shirky.com.

DNA sequencing rates are literally doubling every year.

Of course, the extrapolation has limits. One remembers the old joke that Paul Burnett relates in his "Moore's Law and Hybrids":

> If automotive technology had kept pace with Silicon Valley, motorists could buy a V-32 engine that goes 10,000 m.p.h. or a 30-pound car that gets 1,000 miles a gallon—either one at a sticker price of less than $50. Detroit's response: "OK. But who would want a car that crashes twice a day?"—www.hybridcars.com.

Organic Growth

The third reason that cross-selling is on the rise is that many business leaders in sales and marketing organizations are being tasked with expanding market share *organically* (as opposed to growing externally by merger or acquisition), and as quickly as possible. They are supposed to accomplish this organic growth within the context of markets that are constantly changing: consolidating suppliers (as discussed above), consolidating customers, new capabilities and/or product advancements by competitors, and external market forces that are well beyond a business leader's power to control.

If you look at the models that are used by Wall Street analysts and investment banking firms to judge stock performance, it is clear that these entities give enormous weight to growth (at the expense of all other factors). One of the reasons GE keeps getting rewarded is that despite the fact that it's the world's largest organization, it still finds a way to continue double-digit growth every year. When Wal-Mart or McDonald's announces its results, each includes the category of "same store sales." Building more stores is one way to grow, but some day they're going to run out of intersections.

For many sales leaders in this situation of needing to grow organically, the idea of developing new markets or new clients from scratch is a nonstarter. There simply isn't enough time or enough resources to invest. Most industry analyses show that it costs from five to eight times more to acquire a new customer than to retain a current one. It is widely accepted that the cost of losing a customer must include all the hidden costs of lifetime potential spending and bad press. From a business standpoint then, it makes sense not only to do what's necessary to retain current customers but also to expand relationships with those customers. Many business leaders feel that if a customer relationship is not advancing, then it will soon be retreating. For these leaders, cross-selling strategies represent the only path to achieving the goal of achieving organic growth in the face of such daunting market challenges.

In addition to the obvious appeal for sellers, there are advantages for their customers as well in that they can ostensibly address needs that exist within their businesses simply by tapping more deeply into the capabilities of providers whom they already trust. Customers can also achieve greater economies of scale with key suppliers that help them to reduce several different areas of cost all at once. The *advertised* intent of cross-selling initiatives today often includes real, positive outcomes for both sellers and buyers alike.

WHY CROSS-SELLING FAILS

So why, then, do so many cross-selling initiatives fail? If expanding existing, successful business relationships into new areas is potentially beneficial to both seller and buyer, then why do cross-selling programs rarely succeed at creating sustainable increases in customer wallet share?

Unluckily, cross-selling has gotten a bad name with customers because it is done improperly, indelicately, or just plain ineptly. Christopher Fildes puts it nicely in his November 2002 article entitled "The Big Banks Get Ready to Charge but They Still Need a Bullet-proof Horse" in the *Daily Telegraph* (London): "Cross-selling itself is a familiar business daydream—if only we could sell a buttonhook with every button—and in practice may just make the customer cross." It often does make the customer cross because it is focused more on the selfish desire of the seller to sell than on the needs of the customer; it is not done in the spirit of *mutual benefit*.

Cross-selling initiatives generally fail for three reasons: (1) salespeople are averse to the risk inherent in cross-selling; (2) salespeople get lazy and don't actually *sell* (in the sense of "create value") the new products—they just flog them, doting on features and benefits, or they rely on the strength of their relationship with the customer to sell for them; and (3) the initiative itself is rooted in flawed business logic.

Risk Aversion

Many salespeople are resistant to cross-selling because it is inherently risky. In fact, there is no upside to the original seller for bringing in a colleague; there's *only* risk. If things don't go well, the business they already have is going to wobble a little bit; and if things go fabulously well and they make the cross-sell, there's nothing in it for them. Even if there's some sort of referral fee or commission involved, most sellers view cross-selling as simply not worth the risk of losing a great relationship. It should be pointed out that avoiding risk is selfish, while partnering is selfless.

Of course, that's all based on ill-considered logic and a degree of myopia; it comes from the perspective of things the seller wants to sell, instead of from the perspective of value he wants to create. Thus the way to conquer risk aversion on the part of the original seller (who has the existing relationship with the customer) is by bringing value creation to the fore. Because when you create value, even through a colleague, the differentiation accrues to the whole relationship. So the original seller does win. If genuine value is created, the buyer will naturally benefit and the relationship bonds will grow stronger on all fronts. By approaching it from the standpoint of value instead of selling, the original seller ends up with a much deeper and strengthened relationship.

Inept or Inapt Salesmanship

The way it usually works goes something like this: Company A acquires another company (Company B, let's say)—or a merger takes place. This merger or acquisition dramatically expands

Company A's capabilities and offerings. The leadership of Company A tells its new combined sales force to go forth and sell the new products and services.

Take the banking industry: Bank A is primarily a retail bank with a large mortgage business. It consolidates with Bank B, which sells all the business services—insurance, estate planning, treasury management, and so on. There's a great mirage out there; if salespeople will just trade Rolodexes, they can reach all of the existing customers with all of the new services. And so that's what they do: they just switch lists. Salespeople from Bank A will start calling customers of ex-Bank B and say something like this: "Hi, this is Joe. My friend Bob in treasury services [from former Bank B] suggested I call you. I can offer you . . . ." And then there's great disappointment because no sales are being made.

Well, that's because the customers are solving problems unique to themselves. And there's no guarantee that the new products solve a genuine problem for this customer, or meet a need that the customer actually has. As Fildes put it:

> Cavalry generals in the Great War pined to give the order to charge. This strategy, so they believed, would be decisive, and all that stood in its way was the ineptitude of the War Office, which had not yet succeeded in its attempts to evolve a bullet-proof horse.
>
> Commanders in bank boardrooms know the feeling. The winning strategy, they tell each other, must be to create a universal bank, which would offer every kind of service, in its home market and across the world. The model has been expensively tested but remains unproven, pending the evolution of a universal customer.

And even if selling to the mirage, the universal customer, this is just plain lazy or else maladroit selling, and it will not often result in a sale. How is it wrong? Can we even count the ways? It simply ignores the Boundary Conditions of Communication (buyers value more what they request versus what is freely offered to them, even when the offer comes from a trusted supplier); it ignores the necessity of consultative selling—the necessity of questioning (let alone the correct type of questioning, as discussed in Chapter 8); it fails to connect with the customer on a value level (none of the Client Insight Creators are utilized—never mind the fact that not even a recognized problem is on the table yet!). It fails on so many levels that we probably can't even call it "selling." It seems more like peddling!

Flawed Business Logic

It is undeniable that virtually every industry is enduring some de-gree of commoditization. The flow and availability of information to buyers about prospective suppliers is making it more difficult for sellers to distinguish themselves from their competition. Customer procurement strategies are being designed to force suppliers to compete on one lone criterion—price. The fact is, *sales forces can no longer exist in isolation—they must be an integral part of their own company's value creation and value delivery chain.*

For many firms, the path out of this difficult reality runs straight through their existing customer base. Rather than fight the often unrewarding battle of convincing new customers that they're not only competitively different but *valuable*, these organizations look to expand their relationships with existing customers who seemingly already perceive some value in their capabilities. The very existence of a business relationship seems evidence enough of the kind of perceived value that can be traded like currency in order to get ac-cess to new areas of the customer's business. This is to say, the fact that a client already trusts a seller seems to be evidence in itself that the client would welcome the seller's other capabilities.

Unfortunately, many business and sales leaders who choose to embark on companywide cross-selling initiatives are operating under the flawed assumption that this *currency* is worth a great deal more than it really is. In many cases, it amounts to nothing more than fool's gold.

Ineffective cross-selling initiatives fail because they turn the idea of the *sales force as part of the value creation and value delivery chain* squarely on its head. They frequently pit what is good for the selling organization against what is good for the buyer, essentially forcing sellers to offer expanded capabilities without first helping buyers to gain insight on new opportunities they can seize or challenges they can address.

In its proper orientation, today's business value chain starts from the perspective of the customer. It is for this reason that sellers in today's market have such a vital role in establishing competitive differentiation for their organization. Without the seller functioning as the eyes and ears of a business's value delivery chain, vital functions like product fulfillment, service delivery, manufacturing, and R&D are essentially blind and deaf.

"If we build it, they will come," made for a memorable line in a Kevin Costner film, but it makes for lousy business strategy, unless an organization has somehow combined capabilities in such a way as to create a near-monopolistic hold on a specific market segment. The reality is that these scenarios don't play out often, and when they do, they are fleeting because today's competitors are able to catch up more quickly than ever.

EFFECTIVE CROSS-SELLING

The first job in effective cross-selling is to realize that to broker capability, the proper mindset is not "I've got a truck full of products and I want to sell them all to you." Rather, it's a mindset that thinks in terms of customers with a splendid array of needs, all of which must be effectively communicated within the seller's company, so that the company at large can meet as many of those needs as possible. You start then with the needs that the customer recognizes and then expand in terms of the needs they aren't aware of.

And if you build your cross-selling plan around that idea—of customer problems you can solve or opportunities you can offer— then you're coming from the market perspective. The conversation may go something like this: "You've told me that it's critically important that you maximize the internal rates of return you have on your money, and that it's working at all times. But as the guy who's running Foreign Currencies, you've told me you will not deal with the Far East. Based on that, there's six hours a day that your money is just sitting fallow. I was talking to one of my pals over in Mortgages, and they're showing an average rate of return on overnight money of 32 basis points. Would it be useful if we could take that money, as it was sitting fallow, and move it real-time into mortgage backs, giving you an additional 16 points? Would that help maximize the rate of return you're looking for on the invested capital you have with us?"

So the point is it's not about the money the customer is spending on currency trading. It's about maximizing the customer's return; it's showing the capabilities you have with the money you're already holding. In other words, "As your broker, I may have found a way to make you a little more money. Would you be interested in that?"

HP Financial Services

Hewlett-Packard (HP) is one of the largest consumer products companies in the world. It's an $85 billion company. It has a division called HP Financial Services (HPFS), which provides financing. It sells money. HPFS is one of the arrows in the quiver of brokering of strength of the sales force that represents HP in the marketplace. HP salespeople don't just think, "How can I get this hardware placed with that client?" Instead they think, "How can I get my product into the client's hands in such a way that it has the softest impact on the expense side of that client's balance sheet and income statement? What can we do at HP that allows the client to have the softest impact on cash flow?" So they broker in this financial arm HPFS—even though the client didn't ask for it, and probably didn't know it exists as an option.

FROM CONCEPT TO REALITY: THE STEP-BY-STEP CROSS-SELL

Problem	Solution
1. Risk aversion	Codify "what's in it for me?"
	Internal partnership—intimacy principles.
2. Inept or inapt salesmanship	The confirmation bias is paramount.
	Define vision and impact in client outcome terms.
3. Flawed logic	Realistic mindset.
	Client focus versus seller need to sell.

We've looked at the barriers to effective cross-selling; let's now look at the solutions. Accept at the outset that this is a *selling* job and often not an easy one. Clients, like everyone else, are reluctant to change. They may be very happy with their current suppliers. Your company may be able to offer the same products or services to clients, but they may not be actively seeking a new vendor. And the fact that clients trust you with one piece of their business does not mean that they trust the rest of your products or services. Prepare yourself to *sell*; take nothing for granted.

The first step in cross-selling is to overcome the natural risk aversion that *will* prevent the expansion of the client relationship with the selling company unless it is handled. This is vital because if the original seller can't get past the risk aversion, no effective cross-selling can ever take place.

The risk to the original seller is mitigated in two primary ways. The first is to codify the WIIFM (what's in it for me?) such that the original seller deems the cross-sell worth the risk to his current good relationship with the customer. The only way that the original seller in fact gets anything out of a cross-sell is by basking in the glow of the client's feeling as though the original seller has brought to bear greater value and is likely then to elevate him to trusted advisor status. This of course makes it that much harder for a competitor to unseat him. The second way to mitigate risk is to build intimacy, and trust in particular, within the selling organization. The original seller needs to believe that his colleague from another division (who will benefit from the cross-sell) is not going to wreck his relationship with the client. This becomes possible as the level of trust and intimacy grows. The best way to reassure the original seller that all will be well is by preparing for the cross-sell *together*. The question to ask is this: "What can you—my colleague—do for my client that will make my client better off doing business with both of us, instead of just doing business with me and somebody else that doesn't have any association with us?"

Effective cross-selling is in effect partnering with your colleagues who sell different products or services to produce desirable outcomes for the client. It is about planning together the Unrecognized Problems, Unanticipated Solutions, and Unseen Opportunities that can be brought to bear by the selling company on behalf of the client. The preparation can be done using the same steps we outlined in Chapter 3 on the Unanticipated Solution (see Figure 6.5). It needs to be done in an internal partnership setting. The first step is to identify and prioritize areas where your company's

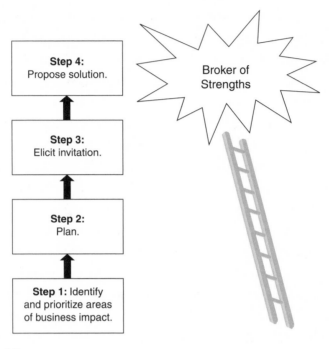

Figure 6.5

capabilities can have an impact on your customer's business, and again, it cannot be done in a vacuum. You need to work in close relationship with your colleagues who handle products and services different than yours. Work out what business impacts they can have on behalf of your customer. And work out why it is a better bet for the client to bring all his business to you.

Then strategize and plan before you make the call. Remember that your customer is most likely already buying the products and services you can offer through your company elsewhere. What the customer does not know is either (a) that your company can offer the solutions too or (b) that the synergy gained from bundling products and services and buying them all in one place can have significant advantages. Your customer may have a natural reluctance to put all his eggs in one basket. Your job is to help him overcome those fears by helping him to discover for himself the scalability, time and effort savings, and so on, to be gained by expanding his relationship with your company.

Use the brokering plan in Figure 6.6 to work out beforehand the kinds of impacts that your company can have on the business outcomes of your client. From this matrix you will plan your call. What questions will you ask to elicit the invitation to propose your company's solution? In this case, your proposal will be to introduce your client to others in your organization who can solve those business issues that your client has already confessed. Perhaps he is unhappy with his current providers, or perhaps you can provide him with economies of scale by meeting a variety of his business needs all under one roof. Remember that the Confirmation Bias is still paramount; the customer must discover for himself the benefit of expanding his relationship with the selling company. Do not flog products and services. Ask questions that lead the

Brokering Plan

		Client Business Functions				
		Revenue	Cost of Sales	Margin	Expenses	Profit
Your Capabilities	Company					
	Products and/or Services					
	People					

Figure 6.6

client to discover better value and thereby greater outcomes. Elicit the invitation.

Once you have elicited the invitation to share your insight, it is time for the cross-sell. Use the opportunity to suggest that perhaps your colleague (from another division within your company) would be well suited to meet the need. Indicate that said colleague can take it from here. Introduce your customer to your colleague, reiterating the aha moment that your customer has had. Make sure that your colleague is very clear about the problem or the opportunity that you have discussed. And then make the hand-off.

BRINGING IT ALL TOGETHER

So, there it is. We have shown you the Client Insight Creators that research has proven to be predictors of success in sales. And beyond just making the sale (which is the technical definition of success), the research has shown that customers are in fact willing to pay a premium—to deliver you from the price war—when these Client Insight Creators are properly employed. There we have the second tool for escaping the price-driven sale. The Client Insight Creators are an excellent roadmap; now we shall teach you to drive. We shall teach you how to *properly employ* them; to execute for success.

Without excellent salesmanship, these concepts will not be leveraged to their fullest potential. Let's now look at how we can bring these Client Insight Creators to life.

KEY POINTS

☞ The individual Broker of Strengths is the seller who can bring to bear the full array of his company's resources on behalf of the buyer to produce for the buyer a more desirable outcome.

☞ Bringing to bear the full capabilities of an organization is achieved through effective cross-selling.

☞ There are several trends that are necessitating cross-selling initiatives across most industries:

1. *Consolidation of suppliers.* Tremendous merger and acquisition activity across the board has opened huge new markets within individual companies, especially banks.

2. *Moore's Law.* There is an ever-decreasing time-to-market for new products.

3. *Organic growth.* Wall Street is increasingly rewarding organic growth and penalizing low growth.

☞ Cross-selling has a bad name with customers because it is most often done improperly, indelicately, or just plain ineptly.

☞ Many salespeople are resistant to supporting cross-selling because it is inherently risky to their relationships with their clients.

☞ The sales function must be the primary driver of value creation and an integral part of the value delivery chain.

☞ Cross-selling initiatives typically fail because they draw the attention of sellers to moving products and services rather than creating value for the client.

☞ The primary objective of effective cross-selling is to establish an approach to customers with an array of needs, all of which must be effectively communicated within the seller's company, so that the company at large can meet as many of those needs as possible.

TURN CONCEPT TO REALITY

In-depth research, case studies, and diagnostics
www.huthwaite.com/escaping

PART 3

EXECUTION

7

ADAPTING TO THE CHANGING MARKETPLACE

It's the sizzle that sells the steak, and not the cow, although
the cow may be mighty important. Steers can't take orders
for their shank bones, but, when the waiter carries a sizzling
steak across the restaurant, you hear, see, and smell that
sizzle—and buy! Find the sizzle in what you sell—and
you'll find success.

—ELMER WHEELER, 1940

WE have seen the new definition of "customer value" in the marketplace. Utilizing the Client Insight Creators, we have seen
what successful salespeople are doing to *profitably* meet the changing needs of the customer. But the question remains, how does the individual seller, and the company for that matter, execute against this
new reality? In other words, what skills are necessary to put the
Client Insight Creators into practice? We've looked at strategies and
tactics; let's now look at the skills that will bring them to life.

Employing the Client Insight Creators properly will require
sellers to adapt to the rapidly changing marketplace realities. The
new sales environment demands a high skill level from successful
salespeople. Strong skills will help to mitigate the ever-increasing
difficulty of selling. We shall look at the requisite skills in a moment.

First, however, we must take a small detour that will help us understand the changing dynamics of the marketplace and the evolution of sales skills to meet new demands. The evolution of sales skills is a most instructive little excursion that will help us put the Client Insight Creators into context as they relate to the changing environment. In short, effective selling skills morph and adapt to the vicissitudes of the marketplace

THE CHANGING MARKETPLACE AND ADAPTIVE SALES SKILLS

As you can see in the timeline in Figure 7.1, changes in the marketplace are speeding up dramatically. The business-to-business sales of the Industrial Revolution have given way to a new kind of reality that's technology driven. The Quality Revolution that began in the 1950s and continues to this day has itself morphed, from a focus on zero defects (product perfection) to a focus on process perfection. The Information Revolution began in the early seventies with the advent of the commercial microprocessor. But already the Information Revolution (powered by hardware) has been superseded by the Knowledge Revolution powered by software. And as we shall see in more detail shortly, PowerPoint and the World Wide Web have fundamentally changed the nature of the marketplace. Writing in the Journal *Innovative Leader* (vol. 12, no. 12, December 2003), Dr. Noel Tichy, in his article entitled "The Knowledge Revolution," states:

> Like the industrial revolution, the knowledge revolution is reordering the ways that people relate to one another and to work. The instant availability of information has broken down the walls separating individuals, institutions and economies. Intangibles have replaced physical goods as the primary source of customer value. And the brains and energy have replaced plant and equipment as the resources most critical to producing that value.

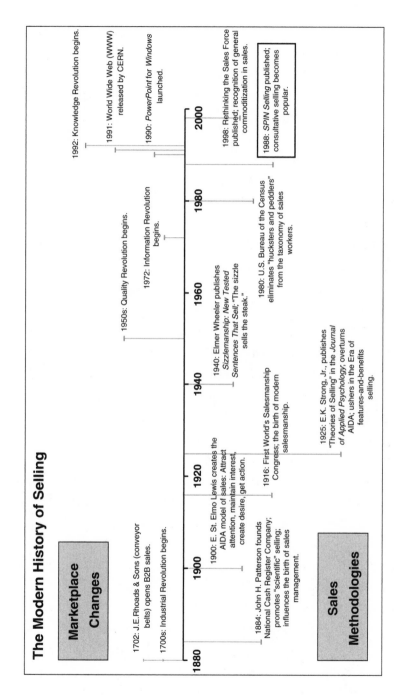

The Modern History of Selling

Marketplace Changes

1702: J.E.Rhoads & Sons (conveyor belts) opens B2B sales.

1700s: Industrial Revolution begins.

1950s: Quality Revolution begins.

1972: Information Revolution begins.

1992: Knowledge Revolution begins.

1991: World Wide Web (WWW) released by CERN.

1990: *PowerPoint* for *Windows* launched.

1998: Rethinking the Sales Force published; recognition of general commoditization in sales.

1988: *SPIN Selling* published; consultative selling becomes popular.

1980: U.S. Bureau of the Census eliminates "hucksters and peddlers" from the taxonomy of sales workers.

1880   1900   1920   1940   1960   1980   2000

1900: E. St. Elmo Lewis creates the AIDA model of sales: Attract attention, maintain interest, create desire, get action.

1884: John H. Patterson founds National Cash Register Company; promotes "scientific" selling; influences the birth of sales management.

1916: First World's Salesmanship Congress; the birth of modern salesmanship.

1940: Elmer Wheeler publishes *Sizzlemanship: New Tested Sentences That Sell*; "The sizzle sells the steak."

1925: E.K. Strong, Jr., publishes "Theories of Selling" in the *Journal of Applied Psychology*; overturns AIDA; ushers in the Era of features-and-benefits selling.

Sales Methodologies

Figure 7.1

Prior to the application of behavioral analysis to the study of selling, salesmanship was not quite regarded as a profession; indeed, it was not highly regarded at all. Think of the old jokes that describe salespeople: "How can you tell when a salesman is lying? His lips are moving!" Or what about the poor "farmer's daughter"?

One thinks of the fast-talking, glad-handing, slick salespeople of yore—and recoils. In fact, it wasn't until 1980 that the U.S. Census Bureau got rid of the occupational classification called "hucksters and peddlers." There was something unctuous about the salesperson that put him several rungs down from the status of true professionals. Of course, it has been said that the oldest profession was a form of selling. But sales has not been regarded properly as a "profession" in the *Merriam-Webster* sense of "an occupation, such as law, medicine, or engineering, that requires considerable training and specialized study" until 20 years ago.

In 1884, John H. Patterson founded the National Cash Register Company. By force of his own inimitable style, he had a major impact on the birth of sales management by creating what amounted to the first highly organized and tightly controlled national sales force. He was not unlike other major manufacturers of the time in that he sought to build a system of sales management that would coordinate production and distribution. It has been argued by Walter Friedman in his compelling book *Birth of a Salesman* (Harvard University Press, 2004) that Patterson almost single-handedly ushered in the techniques of modern sales management.

Modern salesmanship, according to Friedman, was born in 1916 at the first World's Salesmanship Conference in the Arcadia Auditorium in Detroit. President Woodrow Wilson was the keynote speaker, and the stage was shared by a wide variety of businesspeople, academics, consultants, politicians, psychologists, and advertising executives. Together they proclaimed a "new era of salesmanship, in which selling would be conducted according to systematic principles."

In 1925, E. K. Strong, Jr., published an exceptionally influential article called "Theories in Selling" in the *Journal of Applied Psychology* that opened the era of *features-and-benefits selling*. His approach dominated the selling scene until 1988 when Neil Rackham showed that there is a fundamental difference between simple and complex sales. Rackham went on to prove that without *explicit needs* on the table, sales will not be made. He then provided a questioning model to uncover and develop explicit needs, and opened an era of consultative selling. Explicit needs, incidentally, are specific customer statements of wants or desires. Typical examples would include "We need a faster system," "What we're looking for is a more reliable machine," or "I'd like to have a backup capability."

Neil Rackham began an extraordinary research study in 1976 that continues unabated at Huthwaite. The conclusions from the first 12 years of that research were published in his groundbreaking book *SPIN® Selling* (1988). His conclusions fundamentally changed the world of selling. Specifically, it did two things: (1) it further professionalized the practice of sales by setting it on a scientific foundation, and (2) it revolutionized the practice of sales by proving that world-class sellers ask questions of a type made famous by the SPIN model. *SPIN® Selling* and its concepts forever changed the history of selling.

And then, just two years later, PowerPoint for Windows was launched. PowerPoint unleashed two unintended consequences: *description* and *commoditization*. All of a sudden, salespeople had this marvelous tool for describing their products and services. Sales became a description business. And the people who succeeded by describing have become today's business leaders. The problem is that today description is a losing battle (as pointed out in Chapter 1). But we've got a PowerPoint addiction. How many sellers don't use PowerPoint for a demonstration? And what does PowerPoint do but describe, albeit in clever, concise, and sometimes beautiful ways—but it still describes. Genuine conversation between buyer and seller was to a large degree quashed.

PowerPoint not only became the *de rigueur* means of presenting information but it also produced conformation in a format that standardized everything. Salespeople began using the same templates, and everything started to sound the same to the buyer. You really think your clip art is better than the next guy's? PowerPoint was a powerful commoditizing force. In response to that commoditization, an era of value creation dawned.

OK, so that's the history. Now here we are in the present. Changes in the marketplace continue to dictate new ways of selling if success is to be assured. What follows is a glimpse at the present and the immediate future.

THE REALITIES OF TODAY'S MARKETPLACE

The modern salesperson faces three significant marketplace realities today (Figure 7.2). First, the availability of information is unprecedented. The Internet in particular has virtually flooded the world with information, such that the salesperson is no longer necessary to tout form and function of products or services. Second, continuous quality improvement is taking away what was traditionally low-hanging fruit for the consultative seller. Sellers

Realities of Today's Marketplace	Implications for Sellers
Velocity of information ⟶	Salesperson is not needed to simply convey information.
Ever-improving quality ⟶	Less low-hanging fruit.
Accelerated commoditization ⟶	Cannot rely on products to sell themselves.

Figure 7.2

must rely more heavily than ever on the consultative questioning skills that lead to the answers that can be used to create value. And third, commoditization is accelerating at an alarming rate. Products and services are looking more and more alike to modern buyers, who are therefore apt to make decisions based on price alone.

The Velocity of Information

Apace with the advancement of the Web over the past 15 years, customer attitudes toward buying have changed drastically. Before the flood of information availability, customers *had* to see salespeople in order to get information about products and services—or at least it was the quickest and easiest way. The salesperson as talking brochure was in a sense legitimate. Today, that no longer serves. The information is available faster, easier, and cheaper elsewhere—for the most part, right at the buyer's fingertips.

The buyer today is awash in useful information and can solve a vast array of common business challenges with a few mouse clicks. In the recent past that simply wasn't the case. The explosion of information makes it so much easier today to obtain the tools that can solve so many common business problems.

The availability of so much information has now created a general impression of commoditization, even where it doesn't exist. Sifting through and sorting out the torrent of information, everything begins to appear homogenized. Pick any industry, and read the copy from the homepage of the top five companies in that industry. In virtually every case, it begins to blend together. It all sounds the same. It may not be, but it feels like it. Everything begins to look like a commodity. Distinctions blur. And suddenly you find that the customer is interested only in price. In other words, customers who see no difference between options A, B, and C will usually opt for the lowest price.

The Quality Revolution

The second major influence on today's marketplace is the *Quality Revolution*. Over the past two decades there has been a quantum leap in terms of reducing product defects and improving complex processes. Today, products are far more reliable than they were in the recent past—whether it's an automobile or a computer system. Your TV rarely breaks down anymore; your stereo will probably be obsolete before it falls apart; same with your microwave oven.

There is plenty of evidence to suggest that products are getting better and better all the time. Take several data points in varied industries by way of illustration:

- In 1980, owners of 88 out of 100 new vehicles, domestic and import, told *Consumer Reports* that they'd had problems the first year. Today, the number is 16 out of 100, according to Frank Greve in the *Seattle Times*.

- Scout Boats, Inc., is introducing another marine industry first: a new 100 percent manufacturer-backed three-year stem-to-stern warranty on all 2005 and newer models. "With our new warranty, we will be able to give our customers more peace of mind when purchasing a Scout boat," said Vice President of Operations Dave Wallace. "Our boats are built to a much higher standard, so it made sense to back our product longer than any other boat brand in the industry."

- According to *Warranty Week*, warranty claims are averaging close to 1 percent of product sales for 140 U.S.-based manufacturers of medical and scientific equipment and devices. "That could partially be a . . . function of the magnified effect even a minor defect can have on a small company's income statement when *perfection is expected*" [emphasis added]. People are returning medical and scientific equipment and devices that are mildly imperfect simply because they expect perfection and will settle for no less.

The same is true in the business-to-business (B2B) environment, but it's a more recent phenomenon. The new "cyber realities" of constant access, immediate response, connected mobility, process integration, and interface richness have fundamentally changed B2B relationships for the better.

Messrs. Lee, Zuckweiler, and Trim, in the "Modernization of the Malcolm Baldrige National Quality Award," note: "In the USA, quality management became a national concern in the 1980s as many U.S. firms could not compete effectively in the global market, especially in the face of the onslaught of Japanese firms in such critical industries as automobiles, consumer electronics and machine tools. In 1987, the U.S. government launched the Malcolm Baldrige National Quality Award (MBNQA) to recognize firms achieving excellence in quality products and processes. Since then, most U.S. firms and public organizations have implemented various quality programmes, including 44 states."

Interestingly, quality has not improved in the customer's estimation because every quality improvement raises the standard and the customer's expectations of quality rise with it (see Figure 7.3). In other words, as quality improves, the bar is raised in the customer's mind. Customer perception of quality can never quite reach the expectation because expectations are an upwardly mobile target.

"There is no anchor to customer expectations," said Jack West, American Society for Quality (ASQ) past president. "What customers expect today is not what they expected 10 years ago. Successful companies must continually ramp up their quality practices to keep pace with ever-increasing consumer demands."

Expectations and Overall Quality 1997 to Q4 2003

Source: American Customer Satisfaction Index. American Society for Quality, Milwaukee, WI, 2005.

Figure 7.3

Today sellers have two problems related to quality: (1) there is less low-hanging fruit of real quality differentiation, and (2) customers expect more than ever before. The use of methodologies like six sigma, total quality control (TQC), and complex processing has reduced the number of defects per 100,000 units down to a very small amount as compared to 20 years ago. In short, the Quality Revolution, like the velocity of information, has in many ways removed product differences that customers recognize as worth paying for. The bar has been raised so that most companies today have products that are of very high quality. And the velocity of information has supported this trend because now a competitor can get information just as fast as customers can. With the use of modern technology, a competitor can produce the me-too version—perhaps even a slightly improved version—faster than the market can see that it belongs to the earlier brand.

Since the quality of products has risen, the easy differentiators are now much harder to spot. Before the onset of the Quality Revolution in the mid-1980s, it typically took five years in the business-to-business framework for a product to get introduced. Which means it took five years on average for competitors to be able to introduce the competing product. That's a long time to enjoy a feature differentiation.

The cascading impact of product quality in the world of the manager (and especially in the C suite) is that there are far fewer of *today's* problems to solve. And thus managers are no longer paid to solve *today's* problems. Executives and managers are now paid to look over the horizon—to identify opportunity and to anticipate difficulty. It is now much more about the future—and about the competitor—than it is about internal operations. By way of example, consider the recent birth of an entirely new industry, an industry that affects every business that has an IT department, every port, every airport: *homeland security technology*. It is an industry that is *100 percent* about anticipating future difficulties. "Today" we are relatively safe. "Tomorrow" is another story altogether.

So how does this quality improvement affect the twenty-first-century salesperson?

1. It is more difficult for consultative sellers to point out problems with existing equipment, products, and so on.

2. Performance differences between products are less significant, driving commoditization. The low-hanging fruit of differentiation has evaporated.

Accelerated Commoditization

We've already discussed the commoditizing tendency of PowerPoint. The use of templates has trimmed the edges off of differentiation by standardizing presentations across the board. Everyone has the same template; everybody uses the same format: three bullets per page, no more than five words per bullet, similar clip art. We have this pervasive tool that is forcing commoditization.

Indeed, it's one of the great business truisms of our age that products and services are becoming commoditized more rapidly than ever before. Globalization and deregulation and especially the Internet will continue to increase the number of suppliers, with relatively undifferentiated products across a broad number of industries. As a result, customer choice will continue to grow. While this increase of choice is a welcome boon for consumers, suppliers are unlikely to do much celebrating as greater choice results in tougher, more price based buying.

Technological advances are also pushing more sales into the transactional category. It is becoming harder and harder to maintain true product differences. Technology increases innovation potential, but it also greatly shortens the time it takes to copy a competitor's product. Twenty years ago, it was common for complex innovative products to have as much as a two-year lead time before competitors were able to bring me-too versions to market. Today it's not uncommon for the look-alike versions to be out in the marketplace in a matter of weeks.

Author Brian Tracy describes what he calls the "law of obsolescence": if it works, it's obsolete. In other words, every product and service today is already in the process of becoming obsolete by technology and competition. The twenty-first-century seller is facing an increasingly difficult marketplace reality.

KEY POINTS

☞ Changes in the marketplace are speeding up dramatically.

☞ In recent times, the use of PowerPoint has created a world of talking to customers.

☞ Changes in the marketplace continue to dictate new ways of selling if success is to be assured. Figure 7.4 is a glimpse of the realities of today's marketplace.

☞ The buyer today is awash in useful information and can solve a vast array of common business challenges with a few mouse clicks. The availability of so much information has now created a general impression of commoditization, even where it doesn't exist.

☞ Over the past two decades there has been a quantum leap in terms of reducing product defects and improving complex processes. Today, products are far more reliable than they were in the recent past. Therefore, vivid product differentiators no longer exist.

☞ Products and services are becoming commoditized more rapidly than ever before. Globalization and deregulation and especially the Internet will continue to increase the number of suppliers, with seemingly undifferentiated products across a broad number of industries. As a result, customers without an alternative approach by sellers will continue to rely on price as the only means of making a choice.

Realities of Today's Marketplace	Implications for Sellers
Velocity of information ⟶	Salesperson is not needed to simply convey information.
Ever-improving quality ⟶	Less low-hanging fruit.
Accelerated commoditization ⟶	Cannot rely on products to sell themselves.

Figure 7.4

CHAPTER 8

QUESTIONING SKILLS: THE CLIENT INSIGHT CREATOR'S BEST FRIEND

Always the beautiful answer who asks a more beautiful
question.

—e.e. cummings

If you don't ask, you don't get.

—Mahatma Gandhi

FACING TODAY'S MARKETPLACE REALITY

In the context of the Client Insight Creators, we have seen that customers are willing to pay a premium to the seller who provides
insight. We have also seen that there are several marketplace realities
that are making selling more difficult. So how does a seller bring
the Client Insight Creators to life? How does he execute in this complex environment? Our research has shown that we already have the
answer: *consultative selling*. However, the application of traditional

consultative selling is changing with the marketplace. If we understand the changing application of consultative selling through the lens of the current marketplace changes, we will see that exceptional value can be created for the customer. Let's begin by taking a look at the nature of consultative selling.

Modern consultative selling was founded with the groundbreaking research of Neil Rackham and his team. In 1976, Neil Rackham was a behavioral psychologist studying success factors in human relations. He chose to put the world of sales under a microscope because "success" in selling can be measured: the salesperson either gets an advance, makes the sale, or doesn't. The behaviors that end in success are both qualifiable and quantifiable. In other words, sales success factors are testable. Neil Rackham's was the largest and most comprehensive research study ever undertaken to isolate and identify the distinct behavior traits of successful salespeople. The study involved the meticulous observation and analysis of over 35,000 sales calls. The behaviors of more than 10,000 salespeople and 1,000 sales managers from some of the world's leading selling organizations were observed in 27 countries.

We should note that human behavior has not changed. Babies are born every second, but human nature seems to change little, if at all. As Thomas Stewart put it so beautifully in the *Harvard Business Review,* "We find cautionary tales about leadership in Shakespeare; he found them in Plutarch." The behaviors that have been codified as leading to success will always lead to success because human behavior is immutable. Neil Rackham's behavioral studies are as valid today and will continue to be in the foreseeable future as they were nearly 30 years ago. The SPIN model was derived from a study of human interactive behavior. Human interactive behavior, like human nature, doesn't change year to year. What changes is the context in which that behavior is considered appropriate. If you think back a hundred years, the ways in which we displayed courtesy to one another would seem absolutely absurd today. But that doesn't mean that the human being doesn't still extend courtesy; it just means it's done in a completely different context.

What Huthwaite has done every year, through its client engagements, is revalidate and revise the context of application of the SPIN model. We've revalidated the fact that the SPIN model still functions in exactly the same way as it ever did; that eliciting the kind of insightful conclusions and invitations from clients is the best path to selling because that's the human nature element of it that doesn't change year to year. So on the one hand, we could say the 1988 context of the SPIN model is absolutely dated and terribly old, which is why just reading that book may not get you very far anymore. Whereas the model itself—its idea that questions that create discovery in the mind of the customer—is very appropriate. Perhaps more appropriate than ever before.

Behavioral analysis is quantifiable, empirical, and objective. In the science of sales, without that basis, you're relying on guesswork. Do not be misled: rootstock matters. If you're basing everything on anecdote, assumption, or library research, you're missing the real-world element.

There is also the problem of measurement. Without observable and quantifiable behaviors and a scientific method, there's no way to measure sales performance except *ex post facto*; you can establish only lagging indicator measures. Leading indicators can be established only when you know what the indicators leading to success actually are. And the only way to know that is by using large data samples, the scientific method, and behavioral observations. Neil Rackham's 12-year study stands alone in the field. Let's therefore look through the lens of the world's most influential consultative selling model, and keep these points in mind as we examine its modern application.

THE CHANGING CONTEXT OF SPIN

SPIN arguably created the consultative selling industry, and it is still the industry standard. Since *SPIN® Selling* was written, over 500,000 sales professionals have been formally trained in the SPIN methods. They have executed an estimated 9 million sales calls employing SPIN behaviors. Many of the Fortune 500 companies employ SPIN. The effectiveness of the model is undeniable. Many thousands of individual successes, including new sales made, accelerated sales cycles, and revival of transactional relationships, have been documented from companies across every major vertical market. In fact, today sellers are enjoying more success than ever:

- Since the year 2000, over 100,000 observations have been made of salespeople using SPIN during customer interactions.

- Of the participants observed using SPIN behaviors, 91 percent reported tangible business success attributable to these skills.

- Within the first 90 days after learning these new skills, participants on average attributed an increase in revenue of over 12 times the cost of their investment in development.

Asking questions is no longer enough. It's the answers that matter. The questions have to create an aha moment for the customer. You used to have low-hanging fruit; you could point out profound differences in quality and features between products. Today those differences either don't exist anymore or they evaporate before you master them. The half-life of product differentiation is too short to use in the selling process. So you have to find something more sustaining, and finding it is really quite simple because it's applying the same techniques in different ways.

The original SPIN model was used to develop an *explicit need* for the seller's *product or service*. In the new frame of reference, it is *also* used to develop an explicit need for the seller's *expertise*; to create and deliver value for the customer, using one or more of the Client Insight Creators.

What's in a Name?

With the negative connotation that often attends the word "spin" ("spin doctor," "spinmeister," and so on.), clients have asked us whether we can change the acronym SPIN. The answer is yes, we can. The fact of the matter is that the acronym doesn't matter at all; it just isn't the point. Call it BICR if you like (background questions, issue questions, consequence questions, reward questions)—the point is that you're getting to a client's explicit need. It's just a model to get you there. The descriptive words are very flexible.

While the skills necessary to successful selling remain unchanged, the application of SPIN has adapted to the changing marketplace. To understand what's changed, we must begin with the basics of the model itself. *SPIN® Selling* briefly describes the model as follows:

> Asking questions that are important to the customer is what makes the SPIN model so powerful. Its questioning sequence taps directly into the psychology of the buying process. Buyers' <u>needs</u> move through a clear progression from Implied (*statements by the customer of problems, difficulties, and dissatisfactions. Typical examples would be "Our present system can't cope with the throughput," "I'm unhappy about wastage rates," or "We're not satisfied with the speed of our existing process.")* to Explicit. The SPIN questions provide a road map for the seller, guiding the call through the steps of need development until Explicit Needs have been reached (see figure below). And the more Explicit Needs you can obtain from buyers, the more likely the call is to succeed.

Let's briefly review the whole SPIN Model and make a few observations about its use. Most importantly, please don't see SPIN as a rigid formula. It's not. Selling by a fixed formula is a sure recipe for failure in larger sales. Instead, see the model as a broad description of how successful salespeople probe. Treat it as a guideline, not a formula.

In summary, our research on questioning skills shows that successful salespeople use the following general model:

1.   Initially, they ask *Situation* [or *Background*] *Questions* to establish background facts. But they don't ask too many, because situation questions can bore or irritate the buyer.

2.   Next, they move quickly to *Problem* [or *Issue*] *Questions* to explore problems, difficulties, and dissatisfactions.

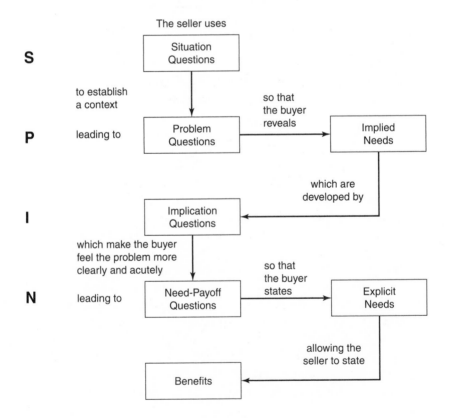

By asking problem [or issue] questions, they uncover the customer's implied needs.

3. Upon identification of Implied Needs, the seller asks *Implication* [or *Consequence*] *Questions* to help the customer understand the severity of the need in a new or different way. They make the implied needs larger and more urgent.

4. Then, once the buyer agrees that the problem is serious enough to justify action, successful salespeople ask *Need-payoff* [or *Reward*] *Questions* to encourage the buyer to focus on solutions and to describe the benefits that the solution would bring.

Of course, it doesn't always work in this sequence. For example, if a customer begins a call by giving you an explicit need, you might go straight to need-payoff [reward] questions to get the buyer talking about how the benefits you could offer would help meet this need. Or sometimes, when you're exploring a problem or its implications, you may have to ask situation [background] questions to give you more background facts. But in most calls, the questioning naturally follows the SPIN [or BICR] sequence. In a nutshell, this is the SPIN Model.

Yesterday, SPIN was an extremely effective way of helping a customer to see problems in a new or different way. SPIN helped the customer to recognize an explicit need for the seller's product or service. Today, that has changed. Of course there must be an explicit need for the product or service on the table, or else there is no basis for a sale, but customers are now trading on the salesperson's *expertise*. The value creation strategies outlined earlier in this book are illustrations of how that insight or expertise plays out in the relationship. SPIN in this new buyer-seller relationship becomes the driver by which value is laid at the feet of the customer. The Quality Revolution has driven out differentiation between products and services; and the Internet has driven out the high premium on information—today the seller has to be able to provide insight. It is *insight* that sustains differentiation. The exchange of goods and services for money happens almost by the way.

The Ugly Truth for Sellers

In recent Huthwaite research, 473 managers were asked, "Which of the comments below would you most likely hear when asking prospective customers for their view of your sales process?" By far the most common answer (39 percent) was, "Their sales team listens to my problems and then shows me which of their menu of products and services can help." Talk about commoditizing your offering! (Incidentally, 90 percent of the managers surveyed recognized that this is not the desirable answer.) Only 4 percent responded with, "They help me explore the depth and scope of issues I didn't even know I had. I feel like I should be paying them for a consultation at the end of each sales call." And that is the language of the customer.

It does need to be said that today's problems have not completely disappeared. There are still genuine problems with genuine implications that can be legitimately explored. But the vast majority of senior managers have neither the time nor inclination to study current problems. The routine problems of the here and now are most often dispatched to lower levels of management for remediation. Indeed, the process for dealing with today's problems has migrated lower and lower on corporate food chains over time. Today's problems are the domain of influencers and implementers. Decision makers concentrate on the future.

You will occasionally find problems that have so far eluded or even defied correction by a hapless manager. That is a lucky day. But be careful not to leap in with solutions (as 63 percent of salespeople are apt to do) before carefully considering all of the implications.

As you can see, consultative selling is getting tougher. To make the Client Insight Creators work, the seller can't be just a talking brochure. Keep in mind the Boundary Conditions of Communication:

1. People value what *they say* and their own conclusions more than what *they are told.*
2. People value what *they ask for* more than what is *freely offered.*

In the preceding chapters, we laid out a roadmap that shows how each Client Insight Creator works. Now we need to learn how to drive. In other words, we need to learn how to execute superior consultative selling skills to employ the Client Insight Creators and thereby mitigate the rapid market changes we've outlined above. Specifically, we have to overcome these hurdles:

- *Velocity of information.* This has raised the bar on asking good questions. Customers expect you to know their business coming in.

- *Quality Revolution.* This has changed the nature of the explicit need (from solving problems to insight). Managers are not paid to solve problems anymore; therefore, problems and implications need to be focused on the five areas of business acumen.

- *Commoditization.* Questioning skills are the only means of avoiding the perception that your product, service, or brand has been commoditized. Creating aha moments earlier in the buying cycle is a must.

So what does all this mean to consultative selling, and in particular SPIN selling? We can sum up by saying that this new selling environment, this new marketplace, has created a chain reaction for consultative selling that has in effect substantially raised the bar on skills. This phenomenon is illustrated in Figure 8.1.

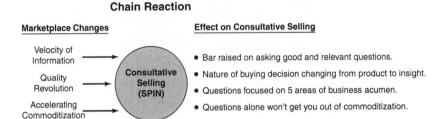

Figure 8.1

As you can see, the velocity of information, the Quality Revolution, and accelerating commoditization are changing consultative selling in four specific ways: First, the bar has been raised on asking good and relevant questions. Second, the focus of an explicit need is changing from product to insight. Third, questions need to be focused on *business outcomes,* or the five areas of business acumen. Finally, questions alone will not get you out of commoditization. We have discussed these realities in different ways throughout the book. Now keep them in mind as we discuss the changes in the application of SPIN.

SITUATION QUESTIONS

Situation questions collect facts, information, and background data about the customer's existing situation. They are designed to create an authentic dialogue with the customer. They demonstrate, if done correctly, that a salesperson has credentialed himself—that he knows something about the customer's company. He's done his homework. In short, they set the context for problem questions; they set the context for the entire dialogue.

If a seller begins by saying, "Bob, you're the head of research here, right?"

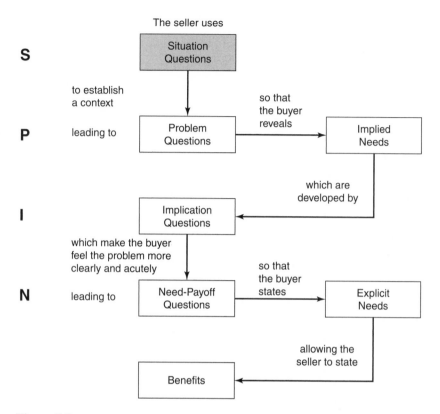

Figure 8.2

"Well, yes," Bob might reply, a bit baffled. Because it's a useless question. It's an irritant because the salesperson should know Bob's title before getting to the meeting.

"And how many people work for you again?"

"Zero."

"Ok, right, zero, got it!"

These kinds of questions are sort of like "What's your sign?" in the bar scene.

On the other hand, if a salesperson says to me, "Thank you for your time. I noted when I was reviewing your last 10Q that there were some interesting things I would contrast with those of your major competitor, and I just wanted to make sure. . . . It says here that your return on sales was 12 percent. Is that actually correct? Did you revise that number?"

That question has an enormous amount of power in it. It's a pure situation question, but it says all kinds of things about the salesperson that couldn't be said with a problem question.

As Neil Rackham points out, you should of course ask situation questions—you can't sell without them. What the research shows is that successful people don't ask *unnecessary* situation questions. They do their homework before the call, and, through good precall planning, they eliminate many of the fact-finding questions that can bore the buyer. *The velocity of information has raised the bar on the quality of situation questions.* The customer expects the seller to know more information prior to the first interaction. Company information, competitive data, and even marketplace data are becoming the rootstock of many situation questions, all of which are easily accessible in the information age. In 1988 (when *SPIN*® *Selling* was first published), it wasn't as easy as it is today for sellers to get good background information. Today a good salesperson can ask a dozen fascinating situation questions, but all of those questions are focused on building the frame in which the salesperson is going to set up for insight delivery.

PROBLEM QUESTIONS

Problem questions probe, not surprisingly, for problems, difficulties, or dissatisfactions. Each problem question invites the customer to state an *implied need*. This implied need may be related to a problem the customer is experiencing or may experience, or it may focus on a better solution or a new opportunity.

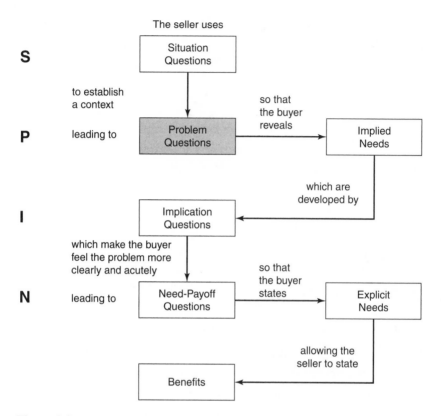

Figure 8.3

Consider now an exercise from which you can develop effective problem questions (Figure 8.4). Problem questions can be classified according to the five business acumen areas we discussed in Chapter 3. In fact, it's a nice starting point. You may have more than one problem question to start with; you can branch out. Look across the areas of the business where you can probe. You may find only a

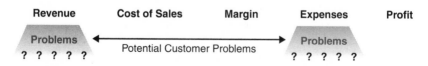

Figure 8.4

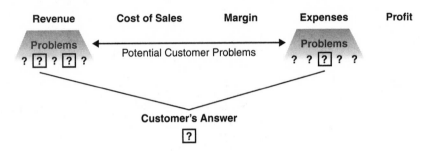

Figure 8.5

few (or even one) business areas in which two conditions exist: (1) there are potential unrecognized problems, and (2) you can positively impact that business area with your solution. Focus on problems you can solve, emphasizing those that are perhaps unrecognized.

Then by careful questioning, boil down your several possibilities to the one (or sometimes several, but that will be rare) that in fact strikes a chord with your customer (Figure 8.5). Your customer will tell you which is the real problem.

Once you've narrowed it down to one problem area, you can begin thinking about that problem through the lens of implications that inevitably must follow (Figure 8.6). It's a way of thinking about problems; it's a starting point.

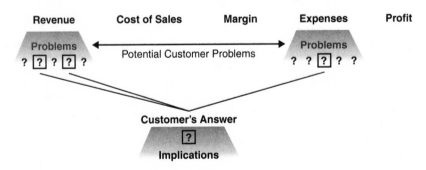

Figure 8.6

Although problem questions are not in themselves sufficient to carry the day, they are nevertheless necessary, for it is the problem questions that provide the raw material on which the rest of the sale will be built.

It's hardly surprising that problem questions have a more positive effect on customers than situation questions do. If you can't solve a problem for your customer, then there's no basis for a sale. But if you uncover problems you can solve, then you're potentially providing the buyer with something useful.

IMPLICATION QUESTIONS

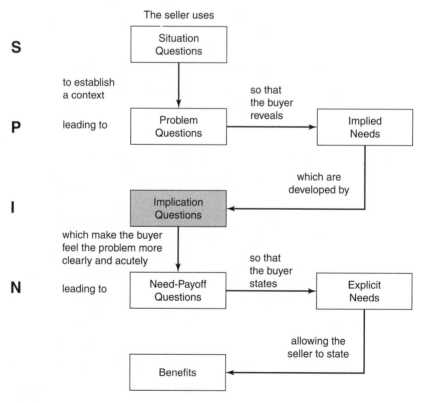

Figure 8.7

Most experienced salespeople, put in front of a major account customer, are able to do an adequate job of asking situation and problem questions. Unfortunately, this is where most salespeople's probing stops. Recent Huthwaite research shows that in 63 percent of sales calls, solutions are offered before the customer states a defined need. If the customer has only an implied need (a need he is not necessarily ready to take action on), then it makes no sense to move to solution. Let's look at an example:

SELLER: *(situation question)* Do you fly executives to corporate meetings?

BUYER: Yes, they always fly first class.

SELLER: *(problem question)* And do they ever have any travel problems?

BUYER: *(implied need)* Well, it can be bothersome when they have to waste a whole day traveling, but it's not the end of the world.

SELLER: *(offering a solution)* We could solve that trouble with a membership in our charter jet club.

BUYER: What does your charter jet membership cost?

SELLER: The package I'd recommend is about $800,000 per year and . . .

BUYER: *(aghast)* $800,000!!! Just to save on some travel annoyances! You must be joking.

What's happened here? The buyer perceives a small implied need—"it can be bothersome"—but she certainly doesn't see that the problem justifies an $800,000 solution. In terms of the Value Equation, the problem isn't big enough to balance the high cost of solving it. But what if the seller had taken a different approach? What if the seller were to focus on the intangibles through the lens of the Client Insight Creators? It's here that implication questions become so important to success. Let's see how a more skilled seller would have used implication questions in this case to clarify for the buyer an *Unrecognized Problem* before offering a solution (in the example, you will also see how the seller ties it to the business outcome of reducing expenses):

SELLER: (*situation question*) I understand from an article I read recently in *Fortune* magazine that your CEO makes $4 million per year and that she does a lot of traveling; is that correct?

BUYER: (*a bit huffy*) Yes, and she flies first class, but she's worth every penny of it.

SELLER: (*problem question*) Assuming she flies out of O'Hare here in Chicago, does she waste much time at the airport, going through security and so on?

BUYER: (*perceiving the problem as small*) Well, of course, everybody does.

SELLER: (*situation question*) I calculate her time is worth approximately $2,000 an hour to the company; do others travel with her?

BUYER: (*still seeing the problem as unimportant*) Yes, and all of their time is valuable, but it's the cost of doing business.

SELLER: (*situation question*) I noticed in your annual report that one of your board meetings was held at Peter Island Resort in the British Virgin Islands—was that a difficult place for board members to get to?

BUYER: (*recognizing a bigger problem*) Yes, it took some board members two days of travel time just to get there! And several of them arrived without luggage. Heads rolled for that fiasco.

SELLER: *(implication question)* How much time and energy did it cost to find and hire a new travel agent?

BUYER: *(seeing more)* It took about a month and cost us quite a bit as we had an excellent relationship with our former agent, and no one seemed to know who was responsible for finding a new one.

SELLER: So it costs the company an average of $2,000 per hour for an average of two hours of check-in and security checkpoint time each time your CEO goes to an airport; and that doesn't include the cost to the company of her entourage. *(implication question)* How much time do you reckon is actually wasted during these vitally important business trips?

BUYER: *(beginning to sense the full brunt of the argument)* Quite a bit, I guess.

SELLER: *(summarizing)* So if your CEO travels extensively, let's say she sees a hundred airports a year conservatively; that's $400,000 in wasted company time just for her! Add the entourage, and the price of the first-class tickets, and we're talking real money. And to be able to make life easier for the board members would have to be a boon to everyone's career.

BUYER: When you put it that way, our executive travel is costing this company a lot more than I would have imagined.

What effect has the seller had on the buyer's Value Equation? What appeared to be a small problem has been put in a new light. It is in fact much larger in the customer's estimation—and much more costly—such that an $800,000 solution no longer seems unreasonable.

This is the central purpose of implication questions. They take a problem that the buyer perceives to be small and explore all of the implications that it leads to so that the buyer gains a more realistic perspective. It becomes, in the customer's mind, important enough to justify action. Implication questions are also used to create the aha moment. They can be used to bring an Unrecognized Problem to light, to uncover the Unanticipated Solution, or to explore the Unseen Opportunity.

Our research has found that implication questions are especially powerful in selling to decision makers. It's often possible to achieve a positive outcome from calls on users or influencers simply by asking problem questions, but with calls on decision makers it's not as easy. Decision makers seem to respond most favorably to salespeople who uncover implications. Perhaps this is not surprising, for a decision maker is a person whose success depends on seeing beyond the immediate problem to the underlying effects and consequences. You could say that a decision maker deals in implications. There have been many occasions when we've been talking to decision makers after a call and heard them comment favorably on salespeople who asked implication questions, saying things like "That person talked my language." Implications *are* the language of decision makers, and if you can talk their language, you'll influence them more effectively.

Implication questions aren't a new discovery. People were asking them long before we began our research. Throughout history, effective persuaders have been uncovering problems and helping others see their full magnitude by exploring their implications. Socrates was a master at doing this—read any of the Platonic dialogues and you'll see how one of the greatest persuaders of all time uses implication questions. However, the case of Socrates also illustrates that, despite their selling power, implication questions have a weakness. By definition, they make customers more uncomfortable with problems. Sellers who ask lots of implication questions may make their buyers feel negative or depressed. Not that many salespeople end up being forced to drink hemlock, but one does wonder whether Socrates' questioning behaviors contributed to his downfall.

Of course, like the days of Socrates, the days of pure problem selling have passed. It is now incumbent on the seller to ask implication questions that lead also to positive discoveries such as the Unanticipated Solution and the Unseen Opportunity. Use the implication question in all of its power; but know that there is another powerful type of question, as follows.

NEED-PAYOFF QUESTIONS

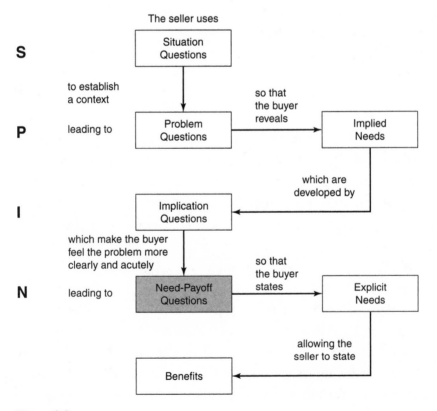

Figure 8.8

Our research at Huthwaite has shown that successful salespeople use two types of questions to develop implied needs into explicit needs. First, they use implication questions to build up the problem (and now the solution and opportunity) so that it's seen in its true light, and then they turn to a second type of question to build up the value or usefulness of the solution: these are positive, solution-centered *need-payoff questions*. Basically, they ask about the value or usefulness of solving a problem, implementing a new solution, or exploring a new opportunity. Typical examples include these:

> Is it important to you to solve this problem? (especially if the problem was previously unrecognized by the customer)
>
> Why would you find this solution so useful? (especially if the solution in question was unanticipated by the customer)
>
> Is there any other way this could help you? (if the customer is seeing a new opportunity)
>
> What's the psychology of need-payoff questions?

- They focus the customer's attention on the *solution* rather than on the problem. This helps create a positive problem-solving atmosphere in which attention is given to solutions and actions, not just to problems and difficulties.

- They get the customer telling *you* the benefits, thereby avoiding cognitive dissonance. For example, a need-payoff question like "How do you think a charter jet membership would help you?" might get a reply like "It would certainly make life easier for the executives and board members." Remember the Confirmation Bias.

Let's see how these objectives are achieved by looking at an extract from a later sales call where the charter jet salesperson is using need-payoff questions to discern the Unanticipated Solution.

SELLER: (*situation question*) As I was flipping through the *Congressional Quarterly* recently, I was struck by a piece of legislation being considered that would dramatically impact your operations. Does your government affairs office have a good relationship with your congressman, and others in that august body?

BUYER: Well, . . . yes, I believe so, but the congressman is very busy; it's hard to get face-to-face time with him.

SELLER: (*need-payoff question*) Would it be beneficial if your CEO could get a couple hours of his undistracted attention?

BUYER: Yes, of course, . . . but that's highly unlikely.

SELLER: (*need-payoff question*) Why would it be important to have undistracted time with the congressman?

BUYER: Because we've had a hard time getting on his calendar, and the legislation you refer to is coming up, and I don't believe he really understands how much it's going to impact his district. It would be great if we could focus his attention on the issues.

SELLER: (*need-payoff question*) Realizing how often a congressman has to come home—for weddings, funerals, holidays, even just weekends—would it make sense to try to get your CEO on a plane with him?

BUYER: Of course. But what are the odds on that?

SELLER: Well, funny you should ask. According to an article in *Bloomberg*, members of Congress can't

> rely on commercial airline schedules because campaign and fund-raising commitments are so demanding. (*need-payoff question*) If you could offer your congressman a discounted ticket to fly on your corporate jet service, and arrange it so that your CEO could fly with him, would that be helpful?
>
> BUYER: Gosh, that's a wonderful idea!

In this extract, need-payoff questions have succeeded in focusing customer attention on an Unanticipated Solution to the problem of getting on the congressman's calendar. Even more important, the customer begins to give benefits to the seller, saying things like "It would be great if we could focus his attention on the issues." It's no wonder our research found that calls with a high number of need-payoff questions were rated by customers as

* Positive

* Constructive

* Helpful

Need-payoff questions create a positive atmosphere in which the customer gives voice to the benefits that will accrue from the Unrecognized Problem, Unanticipated Solution, or Unseen Opportunity that is on the table. We found that this is one reason why need-payoff questions are particularly linked to success in sales that depend on maintaining a good relationship—such as sales to existing customers. Having spoken of the benefits, the customer has made them his own.

The seller that matters is the seller that provides expertise; that expertise matters because it provides insights that wouldn't otherwise be explored. Buyers begin to rely on the dialogue with that seller, as distinct from merely the products and services he has to offer.

Now let's return to the Client Insight Creators, and let's see how they've changed the nature of the buying decision. It used to be that questions could be asked in a straightforward way, looking for the low-hanging fruit of product differentiation or service differences. Those differences have disappeared, as we discussed earlier. So what sellers now need to trade on is their expertise; you need to create an explicit need for your expertise. Consequently, the buying scenario decision is changed to this: "I will buy your product instead of the other guy's because I get expertise from you—and that's the dialogue that I value so much."

Questions alone, even SPIN questions asked around this idea of differentiation probably aren't going to get you very far. The questions that get you out of commoditization are the questions that make you, the seller, different. And you raise the value to the buyer of the dialogue between the buyer and you.

The power of SPIN has not diminished with age; it is as decisive as ever. In the world of consultative selling, SPIN was used originally to develop small problems into large, actionable problems in the eyes of the customer. It was about developing the customer's explicit need. Now, in the world of value selling, SPIN is used to create insights and new forms of explicit needs through the use of the Client Insight Creators. So in some ways, the SPIN model may be even more powerful than it was before.

SPIN is the consummate consultative approach that will bring the Client Insight Creators to life for you; effective questioning skills are the *summum bonum* of your skills arsenal. SPIN is the definitive model that the modern seller can use to counter the rapidly changing marketplace. In fact, the modern seller who does not use effective consultative skills is doomed to commoditization.

KEY POINTS

☞ Too many gurus in the science of selling have failed to do the field research necessary to know what is empirically valid.

☞ *SPIN® Selling* arguably created the consultative selling industry, and it is still the industry standard.

☞ When first introduced, the focus of the SPIN model was to uncover and develop an explicit need in the customer for the seller's product or service. In the new frame of reference the focus is on uncovering and developing a customer's explicit need for the seller's expertise.

☞ The marketplace changes, the velocity of information, the Quality Revolution, and accelerated commoditization have had the following effect on all consultative selling and especially SPIN selling:

1.   The bar has been raised on asking good and relevant questions.

2.   Questions need to be focused on five areas of business acumen.

3.   Questions alone won't get you out of commoditization.

4.   The nature of the buying decision is changing from product to insight.

☞ Therefore, the application of the SPIN model has dramatically changed.

CHAPTER 9

BECAUSE CHANGE
IS NOT AN OPTION

He who rejects change is the architect of decay. The only
human institution which rejects progress is the cemetery.

—HAROLD WILSON

W E have spent the majority of this book describing the four
Client Insight Creators that clients are willing to pay a premium for in today's marketplace. We have also said that the key to
bringing these Client Insight Creators alive is in consultative selling
skills, that is, SPIN. Putting these ideas into action requires behavior change, and effecting change really is a difficult undertaking.
Change happens on two levels: the individual and the organization.
This chapter will show you how to bring these skills to life on both
levels. We'll start with some general comments on change, and then
we'll move on to change and the individual and then to change and
the organization.

Everyone wants progress, but nobody wants change. Change is
difficult, but as Edward Gibbon points out in his monumental
History of the Decline and Fall of the Roman Empire, "All that is
human must retrograde if it does not advance." In our research we
have discovered that change is extremely difficult both for individuals and for organizations. In this chapter we will examine what is

necessary to take the behaviors discussed in the previous eight chapters and convert them into lasting changes whether you are managing yourself as an individual or you're managing a sales team or you're running a company.

Changing behavior can't be accomplished just by reading a book. Even a good book. We are like the doctor who says, "If you want to get in shape, if you want to have a healthy life, then you need to eat right and work out every day." Everyone knows it, but very few people stick to it. It doesn't seem to be a question of people not knowing what to do; rather, it seems to be a question of their not being willing to put in the requisite work. And it's the same both for the individual and the organization. It takes consistency, it takes practice, and it takes doing the right thing every day.

The thing about change is this: It happens. You must respond to it. Darwin noted that it is not the strong that survive but those most adaptive to change. The great longshoreman philosopher Eric Hoffer put it beautifully when he said, "In times of change, learners inherit the Earth, while the learned find themselves beautifully equipped to deal with a world that no longer exists." General Eric Shinsheki pretty much summed up our viewpoint: "If you don't like change, you're going to like irrelevance even less."

THE FOUR TRUTHS OF PERFORMANCE CHANGE: THE INDIVIDUAL

Huthwaite has spent considerable time looking at two areas of human performance research: (a) the principles of adult learning and (b) the latest research into effective change management. An interesting conclusion emerges from the juxtaposition of these two bodies of research. Together they indicate that trying to improve

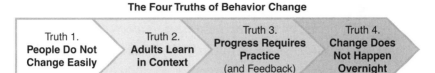

Figure 9.1

one's own performance or improve the performance of an organization will always fail if it relies on the simple transfer of
knowledge— that is, reading a book or participating in a classroom
training session. Achieving a measurable, tangible, and significant
change in sales performance involves far more. It must incorporate the four truths of creating lasting behavior change depicted in
Figure 9.1.

- *Truth 1.* People do not change easily. As the Apostle Paul so
  alarmingly put it, "I do not do what I want, but I do the very
  thing I hate." People are naturally averse to change and find
  it very difficult, for these reasons: the *law of first knowledge*
  prevents them from adapting easily; change requires hard
  work, and people tend to be lazy; and people usually assume
  that the way they are doing something is the best way to do it.

- *Truth 2.* Adults learn in context. That truth rests on a well-
  established principle of androgogy, or adult learning, which
  is that adults are relevancy oriented. They need to be able to
  contextualize a new subject within their own framework in
  order to internalize it.

- *Truth 3.* Progress requires practice (and feedback). When
  attempting to change a behavior or inculcate a new one, there
  is no substitute for practice, repetition, and reinforcement.
  Expertise takes many forms, but it never comes without hard
  work.

- *Truth 4.* Change does not happen overnight. Patience is a virtue. Change takes time. Be prepared. Permanent behavior change requires some form of metrics so that you can judge empirically how far you have progressed. Seeing interim results along the way will help you establish a new behavior.

There is a wide array of myths floating about that purport to have the answer to excellent selling. Unfortunately, these myths tend to be rooted in experience (which is most subjective) rather than scientific research, behavioral psychology, or adult learning theory. Our 30 years of experience in helping sellers change their behaviors has proven that most sellers, with the proper guidance, can make a dramatic improvement in their performance by incorporating some fundamental concepts that are resident within the four truths of behavior change.

Are you prepared to change? The change we are talking about is a behavioral change; it is not as much about new knowledge as about new behavior. You will have to give up the familiar. You are both the change agent and the subject of change. Your job has become doubly difficult because you have to be the one that's driving the change to the very person it's difficult to get to change. Therefore, you have to take yourself through these steps:

1. *Memorialize why you are changing.* What is the measurable outcome you want to produce?

2. *Prepare for the change process.* You're going to have to have the courage and commitment to measure results—are you ready?

You've seen the results from national weight-loss chains, and actually, losing weight in a public setting is the perfect metaphor for most behavioral change processes. You set a goal for yourself, and you go in at regular intervals and stand on the scale—an absolute measure of progress or no progress. By doing it in public, you have a built-in system of rewards and consequences, which is the key to everything. If you lose weight, everybody cheers. If you don't or, worse yet, if you gain weight, you'll be very embarrassed. There's also the built-in reality of whether you were true to the system or not. If you had obeyed the rules, you would have lost weight. If you gained weight, it means you cheated.

Truth 1. People Do Not Change Easily

People don't make changes easily. Human nature makes acquiring new behaviors a difficult challenge. If you don't believe this, just ask a middle school teacher, an exercise coach, a prison reformer, a psychotherapist, or a nutritionist. There are three basic reasons that people don't quickly embrace change:

1. According to the *law of first knowledge*, people continue to believe whatever they learned first, regardless of later evidence against it. This has to do with belief.

2. Most people are not willing to sweat for excellence, which is to say, most people are comfortable with average.

3. People assume that the way they are doing things already is the right way to do things. This has to do with behavior.

The law of first knowledge is perhaps the most powerful enemy of change. Psychologists tell us that we have a tendency as human beings to associate the truth with the first thing we learned. On any new subject, what you learn first becomes truth. We developed this way because when we all lived in caves, it paid to learn fast. The fact is, when we lived as cavepeople, we were pretty low on the food chain, and as a prey animal you don't get a lot of time to make adjustments. You have to learn pretty quickly. Scientists also tell us that we traveled in extended family groups—between 15 and 30. So the law of first knowledge can be seen clearly if our family is out on a hunt one day (or a nuts-and-berries-gathering quest) looking for food and grandma gets eaten by a saber-toothed tiger. The question is, what did we have to learn real fast? Exactly—Always hunt with the elderly. It paid to learn fast. Second thing, always run faster than grandma. And third, tigers are bad. It is in our DNA to adapt quickly because in the early days, we got very few chances.

Another famous example of the law of first knowledge is the Maginot Line in France. The Maginot Line was a massive line of fortifications along the Franco-German border that France had built by 1939 to defend itself against German attack. Static defense in World War I had been successful. The French had learned that attacks from Germany were a Bad Thing, and so they based their entire defensive strategy on a great line of fortifications. In 1940, Germany attacked through Belgium, the Netherlands, and the Ardennes Forest—entirely circumventing the Maginot Line. Generals are notorious for their tendency to fight the previous war.

The fact of the matter is that the law of first knowledge has impact on us as businesspeople all the time. What comes first is always assumed to be true. It takes a lot of evidence to change our minds. And believing is seeing. If you began your career in sales, if you succeeded on the idea that your quality products and your innovative services were what got you value in the eyes of your customers and clients—if that's how you escaped price-driven selling before—then perhaps you should just do more of it. It's a losing battle. You're actually sinking deeper in the quagmire of price-driven selling. To be a great seller in the modern context, you need to learn the Client Insight Creators, and put them into practice.

The reason that people don't like to sweat for excellence is obvious: it is hard work. Few people relish the idea of leaving their comfort zone. There are of course exceptions that prove the rule, for example, extreme sports enthusiasts. But the fact is that most of us have a natural bias for the status quo. Change upsets our routine. It's like the working-out scenario—everyone knows that working out regularly would make them healthier, but few have the discipline to sweat it through. Hence the national obesity epidemic. The other reason that people avoid sweating for excellence is the *motivation dip*: because results are not always immediately apparent, we get discouraged and quit trying. We live in a society that preaches instant gratification. Unhappily, change takes time.

As you can see in Figure 9.2, the level of enthusiasm changes during the learning process. There are usually three stages in developing a new habit: (1) the *"new-toy" stage* during which you are all excited about trying out a new behavior (like a child who gets a new toy on his birthday); (2) the *learning stage,* which is hard work, and during which your motivation is likely to dip; and (3) the *effectiveness stage,* which you will reach if you persist and during which you will begin to see real results.

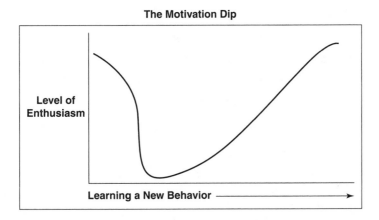

Figure 9.2

The Bad News is that you *will* experience a motivation dip. When you change anything, you are neither comfortable nor good at it the first time you try it. You need to plan on weathering the storm. Think about what happens when people take up a new sport or hobby. At first they are so motivated that they can't talk about anything except their new enthusiasm. Then, when the magic wears off and is replaced by the need for hard work, most people experience this real dip in their motivation level. Fortunately, if you grin and bear it, the Good News is that it doesn't last. Your new behavior will finally prove itself by showing payoff that greatly outweighs effort.

People believe that whatever they are doing already is the right way to do things. People filter out evidence that says they're not doing the right thing. This truth is based on the Confirmation Bias we have already discussed in this book. It can be differently stated as the tendency to search for or interpret information in a way that confirms one's preconceptions. Another cognitive bias that plays here is the *observer-expectancy effect*, which occurs when a researcher expects a given result and therefore unconsciously manipulates an experiment or misinterprets data in order to find it. All of us have a tendency to see only the things that confirm what we already believe. As John Kenneth Galbraith so aptly put it: "Faced with the choice between changing one's mind and proving that there is no need to do so, almost everyone gets busy on the proof." That's why data are so powerful. It's not that we try things and they don't work; it's that we don't try them because they're hard.

Truth 2. Adults Learn in Context

It is a fundamental principle of adult learning theory, pioneered by Malcolm Knowles, that adults are *relevancy oriented*. They need to learn in context. They need to understand the reason that they are learning something. That means they need to see the applicability of the learning to their job. When they do understand the relevance of a new skill set to their work or other responsibilities, adults can learn remarkably efficiently.

The other basic principle is that adults are practical. They want to see a direct line to results. You probably read with great assurance and understood the Client Insight Creator chapters earlier in this book. Have you stopped to consider their application in your specific industry? Ask yourself these questions:

* If someone were to say, "What are the most common Unrecognized Problems of your customers?" would you be able to answer that question?

* If someone were to ask you, "What is the most typical Unanticipated Solution customers find of value?" would you be able to describe that solution?

* Do you know how to describe your company's multiple capabilities in terms of the problems they solve and the opportunities they create for your customers rather than in the products you present to the marketplace?

If not, you haven't put the Client Insight Creators into context. Let us encourage you to stop reading now and go through the exercise of figuring out the answers to those questions. At www.huthwaite.com/escaping, we have a tool to help you lay this out quickly and easily.

It is imperative that individuals seeking change create a clear line of sight between the skills they are being asked to learn and the relevancy of those skills to their daily work. In the case of the Client Insight Creators, it is important that you get a chance to see these skills in action—to see them work. In order to do this, you need to go through the exercise of defining what you actually bring to the table. You need to work out potential Unrecognized Problems, Unanticipated Solutions, Unseen Opportunities, and Broker of Strengths (cross-selling) possibilities. Then take these and practice them, preferably with a colleague or a manager who can role-play with you and give you feedback. You really need a hands-on experience in order to see why it matters that you learn these new behaviors. You need to see the applicability of the Client Insight Creators in the context of your work. And then you need to practice, which systematically enhances learning from experience.

In his book *Patterns of Learning* (San Francisco: Jossey-Bass Publishers, 1984), Cyril O. Houle stated: "Work is the center of most people's lives. By contemplating, analyzing, and improving it, they often discover ways to achieve personal fulfillment and growth." He conducted one of the most famous studies on what motivates learners. One of the principles he identified to categorize motivational styles was that goal-oriented learners use education to accomplish clear-cut objectives. Back to the line of sight then, it is vitally important to see the power of the Client Insight Creators in the context of your own day-to-day business. And to do this, you need to put them in context by actually working out the specifics that you need to learn in order to execute in the field.

Truth 3. Progress Requires Practice (and Feedback)

> When you are not practicing, remember, someone somewhere is practicing, and when you meet him he will win.
>
> — ED MACAULEY

"[If there are any who believe] that those who perform at high levels can do so without extensive practice, they should suspend their belief," said Howard Gardner in *American Psychologist* in 1995. The fact is that practice is the root of gain. There are many schools of thought regarding the nature of expertise: Is it a matter of innate capabilities, raw talent, or natural gift; does it come by learning; is it strictly a matter of temperament? Who perseveres when the going gets tough and why? Regardless of the biology or psychology behind the concept of expertise, everyone agrees that nobody on the planet can improve in their chosen domain without practice.

A word we like to use is *entelechy*, the becoming actual of what was potential—turning something into practical usefulness as opposed to theoretical elegance. Success in any skill—whether in golf, playing the piano, or selling—rests on concentrated, tedious, and frustrating practice. Mahatma Gandhi once said that "an ounce of practice is worth more than tons of preaching."

It is important to note that you need to practice the right stuff. It is no good going to the practice range and whacking golf balls all day long if your grip is wrong or your backswing is too fast. You'll just get very good at a bad swing. So you need practice with feedback. You need coaching. Even from a peer or colleague, if your manager doesn't have time. It is a simple truth that you cannot see your own swing. Even Tiger Woods needs and gets feedback.

With regard to the Client Insight Creators, practice has a special purpose. Practice is about forcing yourself through the process of thinking about how you can employ these Client Insight Creators. What are the kinds of questions you can ask? What are the kinds of call plans you can put together that start first with your understanding of the customer? Once you have correct knowledge, practice your questions on a pal. Role-play occasionally with your manager. Play from a sheet of music that accurately reflects the kinds of situations you can impact on your customer's behalf. And then practice. The great thing is to create habits.

Allene Kieffe describes it this way in his article in the *Grand Rapids Business Journal* (10454055, vol. 18, no. 30, July 24, 2000) entitled "Innovation Is Name of Current Game": "Habits are time savers, allowing the mind to focus on things other than the specific activity being performed. If we had to concentrate on every activity with the concentration required by new behavior, life would be excruciatingly difficult. Imagine having each time you get behind the wheel be just like the first time. Because they are so useful, habits are hard to break, to unlearn, and . . . individuals have difficulty unlearning." In an article called "The Formation of Habits" at www.difficult.ca/Article/IV-The-Formation-Of-Habits.html, the author has this to say:

> The fact of learning depends physiologically on the plasticity of the nervous system. The neurones, particularly those concerned with intellectual life, are not only sensitive to nerve currents but are modified by them. The point where the greatest change seems to take place is at the synapses, but what this modification is, no one knows. There are several theories offered as explanations of what happens, but no one of them has been generally accepted, although the theory of chemical change seems to be receiving the strongest support at present. There can be no disagreement, however, as to the effects of this change, whatever it may be. Currents originally passing with difficulty over a certain conduction unit later pass with greater and greater ease. The resistance which seems at first to be present gradually disappears, and to that extent is the conduct modified. This same element of plasticity accounts for the breaking of habits. In this case the action is double, for it implies the disuse of certain connections which have been made and the forming of others; for the breaking of a bad habit means the beginning of a good one.

There are lots of opinions on what it takes to habitualize a behavior, but one thing is certain: It takes more than one iteration. You have to do it over and over again, with feedback.

Truth 4. Change Does Not Happen Overnight

There is an old proverb that says it doesn't work to leap a 20-foot chasm in two 10-foot jumps. In our case, however, progress is incremental. Do not be alarmed if you don't see immediate total success. Change takes time, perseverance, and effort.

People don't make changes suddenly: you've got to look for incremental success and incremental progress in your own change. The best way to get feedback on how you're actually doing is from your customers and prospects. Just ask them. Ask your most recent customer, garnered from a successful final sales call. Ask her flat out: "Would you have paid a consulting fee for that last call? Did I create real value for you?" And ask those who chose someone else to do business with: "Where did I fail to create value? Would you describe my tactics as a salesperson as consultative? How can I improve my approach?"

Take the feedback and incorporate the learning you derived into your repertoire. Take the feedback, divide it into categories, and then set priorities. Take an action item from each piece of feedback. Figure out where you have made an impact; construct the pattern and file it away for future use. Practice it.

> All conservatism is based upon the idea that if you leave things alone, you leave them as they are. But you do not. If you leave a thing alone, you leave it to a torrent of change.
>
> —G. K. CHESTERTON

But possibly the most important factor here is the absolute necessity of metrics. You have to have some sorts of measures that will help you determine if you are getting any better. In all the games we play, we keep score. And in team sports we keep all kinds of stats. Practice leading nowhere is just a waste of time. You could practice hitting one key on the piano 140,000 times, but you wouldn't be any better at playing the piano.

There has to be some ability to quantify what you're doing. Some examples of the kind of metrics you can establish for yourself as an individual salesperson might be the following:

- Keep track of the ratio of advances to sales calls. If you are genuinely getting better, that ratio should improve dramatically over time.

- Keep track of the number of deals you're getting transactionally, and those in which the price is not the only decision criteria. The lower that ratio, the better off you are.

This is too voluminous a discussion for the purpose of this book, but for more information, visit our Web site at www.huthwaite. com/escaping. There you will find tools that will show you where you are on this journey and what it will take to get you to the ranks of the world-class seller. If you're not keeping some sort of metrics, you can reassure yourself that you're doing better but you very likely may be incorrect.

The science of change is very difficult. Here's a recap of some of the main points that we've talked about. Follow these few thoughts and you'll be on the road to more hopeful change.

People do not change easily.	• The law of first knowledge will prevent easy change. You are hard-wired to believe the first thing you learned.
	• People don't like to sweat for excellence because they are satisfied with average.
	• People assume that whatever they are doing already is the right way to do things—and so are unlikely to desire change.

Adults learn in context.	• Adults are relevancy oriented; they need to see things in context.
	• Adults are practical; they need to know why something matters to them personally.
	• Line of sight is key to contextualization.
Progress requires practice (and feedback).	• Practice the right stuff. It will pay off.
	• Practice has a special purpose—it turns goodness into greatness.
Change does not happen overnight.	• Feedback is vital to keep you on the right path.
	• Metrics are imperative if you hope to see empirical evidence of successful behavior change.

The juxtaposition of the principles of adult learning and the latest research into effective change management indicates that improving performance on a permanent basis requires far more than the mere transfer of knowledge. It requires the willpower to overcome natural psychological biases; it requires dedication and perseverance; it requires practice, feedback, and, perhaps most importantly, measurement. But take courage: it can be done.

THE FOUR TRUTHS OF PERFORMANCE CHANGE: THE ORGANIZATION

Change at the organizational level is like change at the individual level, with a few additional considerations. Interestingly, these truths, while critical to the success of any performance improvement initiative, have little to do with the content of what is being taught. They have everything to do with whether or not the initiative produces results.

Let's look at each of these more closely to understand why so many improvement initiatives fail and how these truths can be harnessed to produce spectacular and inevitable success. Senior leaders are paid to achieve desirable but not inevitable results. Employing the Client Insight Creators on an organizational basis involves changing the way the client interaction function works. That means changing behavior, and therefore there are some fundamentals that have to be appreciated at the organizational level evocative of what we just talked about with the individual (Figure 9.3).

The Four Truths of Behavior Change

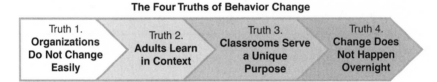

Figure 9.3

- *Truth 1.* Organizations don't make changes easily, nor do they make changes on demand. Only those things that are measured will get done; the engine of change is measurement.

- *Truth 2.* Adults learn only in the context of what they judge to be important and relevant to them as individuals. Just because it's good for the company does not mean it will necessarily be embraced by individual salespeople.

- *Truth 3.* Classrooms serve a unique purpose. Spending time in classrooms is an expensive proposition. Therefore, classroom time should be devoted to the kinds of learning that require interpersonal practice and feedback.

- *Truth 4.* Organizations don't make changes suddenly. Success will come only from an initiative that nests training experience in a process that includes reinforcement, coaching, and quantified, objective, individualized feedback.

As many sales leaders and senior managers have found, getting salespeople to inculcate new behaviors is a very challenging task. Why is it so difficult? Huthwaite has found two issues that cause organizational transformation to fail, as illustrated in Figure 9.4.

Imagine being quite ill and going to the doctor for some relief. You step into the dreaded room, and note that the doctor throws a cursory glance in your general direction and then begins furiously scribbling a prescription for you. You might wonder just what on earth he thinks he's basing his diagnosis on—you haven't even begun to describe your symptoms yet. Prescription without diagnosis is malpractice. To what extent does your sales leadership or training department write the prescription before they really understand the problem with the sales force? Huthwaite has a long and storied tradition of making correct diagnoses for Fortune 500 companies based on *data, not guesswork*. Many of these companies have been surprised by the diagnosis we have performed before we helped them with a change initiative.

Most of what we've covered in this book is dependent on superior selling skills. Is your organization up to the challenge? By reading this book, you've made the important first step in the journey toward improving your sales results. Now comes the hard

1. Diagnosis based on guesswork, not data.

2. Vision alone does not create outcomes.

Figure 9.4

part: making it work every day with your customers. Begin by focusing on *data, not guesswork*. Few executives recognize the magnitude of the challenges of changing an organization in a positive way. Most don't even recognize the categories of challenges, let alone the magnitude. A vision for success, by itself, does not create outcomes. To get a sense for what these challenges entail, and the magnitude of the task facing you in particular, see our Web site to take an assessment of your sales team. We think you'll find your discoveries most compelling.

Truth 1. Organizations Don't Make Changes Easily or On Demand

The most common failure point in most change efforts is that organizations do too little preparation before launching an improvement initiative. Most improvement initiatives are poised to fail from the very start because senior managers *assume* everyone is "on the same page." Unfortunately, tacit understandings (even if they exist) are never strong enough to underpin the effort it takes to change performance.

There are two things that an organization must have in place prior to the first salesperson's being asked to learn something new. First, the company's senior sales leaders must agree on what success looks like. Too often, companies employ outside resources to deliver performance improvement without having codified the differences in how they want the sales force, the sales numbers, or the overall organization to look after the initiative has been launched. Ideally, this definition of success should include agreement on the specific aspects of the business or the people that will show measurable improvement, and the time frames in which these improvements will be recognized. Wherever possible, distinct short-, mid-, and long-term impacts should be delineated. Unless sales leaders agree on what target the initiative is shooting for, there is little chance that anyone will hit the bull's-eye.

The second thing that needs to be accomplished in the initial phase of a change initiative is the identification of a set of metrics that will be employed to drive the initiative over time. *Only those things that are measured get done.* These measures need to be selected so that every level in the organization is responsible and accountable for moving some number or set of numbers in a positive direction over time.

An important factor in this regard is setting metrics that establish a balance between *efficiency* and *effectiveness.*

When most business leaders hear about metrics, they naturally gravitate to accounting measures: ROI, revenue, cost of sales, profits, and so on. Though these kinds of measures are a valuable part of financial management, they are generally not granular enough to be good drivers of change, particularly where sales force behavior is the focus of a change effort.

In the quest for more surgical measures, many executives default to activity-driven measures such as calls per week, sales proposals per month, or call reports per quarter. Huthwaite refers to these kinds of measures as "efficiency metrics." Though these may have a place in driving change, they by no means deliver the full force of measurement. Measures of *effectiveness* are equally important.

Effectiveness measures are those metrics that track how well an individual or an organization is executing those things that are known to be predictive of sales success. Not only do they need to be predictive of success but wherever possible, they also need to be measurable in an objective, quantified, and empirical way. Another way of thinking of these kinds of measures is to recognize that effectiveness measures form leading indicators of success, where often accounting and efficiency measures offer up lagging indicators of success. By having both leading and lagging measures, the processes of midcourse corrections, coaching, and fine-tuning all become more powerful as time goes on.

Truth 2. Adults Learn in Context

Adult learners have many (often unconscious) mental filters. These filters test for relevance and importance. How often has it happened that you were reading interesting material and telling yourself how much you wanted to remember it, only to find that you had quickly lost much of it?

If salespeople are to learn a new set of behaviors, new skills, or new processes, it needs to be presented in the context of their day-to-day experience on the job. It is not enough to introduce concepts, tools, or skill sets in some generic framework and then expect the salespeople to translate these to on-the-job executions.

When a sales performance improvement initiative requires salespeople to do something differently, the learning experience needs to be delivered in a context that matches their day-to-day reality. This means that learning a new set of sales *skills* must involve role-playing and exercises that feel like real sales calls. New *tools* must be introduced in the context of actual account data. New *processes* need to be presented within a realistic framework of company culture and values.

Our research provides powerful evidence that only about 10 to 15 percent of the people who go through sales training will adapt general or generic ideas into their specific day-to-day job performance. It is doubtful that business executives will knowingly invest in any initiative where ROI rides on a mere 10 percent of the participants. In reality, tens of millions of dollars are spent each year on just such kinds of initiatives because too little attention is given to establishing a clear, relevant context for the participants.

Truth 3. Classroom Time Is Expensive If Not Used Properly

Taking Job's four-hour correspondence course on patience does not make a person patient. Therein lies the reason it's more difficult to train salespeople in a few hours than in a couple of days.

In principle, you could take a couple of hours and transfer the *knowledge* of what it is that makes excellent salespeople versus average salespeople. And you could in theory implement that in your sales organization. But the problem is that it puts enormous pressure on the people who would be coaching those who were so "trained." Unfortunately, coaching tends to be the Achilles' heel of most sales organizations. How many sales managers don't get trapped into simply becoming more important salespeople as opposed to sales coaches? Coaching is the thing that's hardest to embrace when you're looking for a sales culture or a sales culture change. So the more pressure you put on the necessity of coaching, the less likely it is you're going to produce an outcome from sales training.

The four-hour training during which you simply transfer information puts 100 percent of the pressure for generating an ROI on the very weak point of most sales organizations: sales coaching. Well-done sales training provides the salesperson with (1) an opportunity to practice the skills for the first time in a safe environment, and (2) immediate, professional feedback. This greatly reduces the amount of pressure on the sales coach, because the salesperson then takes the baton once he leaves that classroom. According to our research, without coaching, participants in training lose 87 percent of what they learned within the first 30 days.

Anyone who has budgeted for classroom training is probably all too familiar with how expensive classroom time can be. Adding opportunity costs from time-out-of-field costs, travel costs, and costs of the training itself to the overhead associated with classroom training produces a total cost figure that scares most executives into the "there's no way our budget can afford it" response. No other factor has contributed more to the meteoric rise in e-learning than the dream of shaving many of these costs.

Unfortunately, when it comes to learning new skills and behaviors, there is no substitute for a classroom experience. No one learns to play golf or tennis without some opportunity to hit the ball. Few people can learn to tango alone. Whether its martial arts, playing a musical instrument, or learning new selling behaviors, the learner must have an opportunity to practice the skill in a safe and nonthreatening environment. In addition, learning a skill always requires some level of coaching. It is impossible for even the most senior and experienced practitioner to simultaneously employ a skill and effectively analyze how to improve. Only classrooms can provide a platform for both safe practice and immediate feedback. Therefore, a classroom is an expensive venue for training, but there is no better way to provide realistic practice and immediate personalized feedback. To effect change, it is essential that training be designed to maximize practice and feedback opportunities.

Truth 4. Organizations Don't Make Changes Suddenly

Truth 1 emphasizes the importance of measurement as the driver of change. Even where appropriate metrics have been established, however, there can be a lack of resolve to employ them over the course of time. There are as many initiatives that fail in this regard as there are failures caused by a lack of measurement altogether. Let's examine some of the key issues to maintaining a focus on metrics and how to prevent a loss of momentum.

Many studies have proven that performance initiatives usually create a momentary drop in performance before positive results begin to show up. Consider, for example, the short-term negative impact we experience when trying a new grip on a racket, bat, or golf club, wearing a new kind of running shoe, or trying a new ball-handling technique. Sales training is the same: New techniques, skills, or tools often impede before they improve sales performance. Too often this momentary dip in performance results in the organization abandoning its commitment to measurement. Once the engine of metrics is shut down, it is only a matter of time until people return to their old way of doing business.

One key to addressing this problem is to establish some form of coaching expectation. Usually, though not necessarily in every case, first-line managers adopt the role of coach. Huthwaite's research has proven that to achieve sustainable sales improvement, having managers serve as coaches is essential.

The two fields where coaching is most often a part of performance improvement are sports and the arts. Interestingly, in either sports or the arts, it would be unthinkable to employ a coach who had never studied the science of coaching. It would be considered even more absurd to hire a coach who was unfamiliar with the techniques and science of the sport or activity she was being directed to coach. Surprisingly, no such standard seems to exist for sales managers. Most managers, if their organization even embraces coaching, are simply told to "coach their people." No one tells them how to coach nor how coaching will be measured. Further, with regard to sales training initiatives, managers are seldom even asked to master the new material themselves. It is as though the organization expects salespeople to emerge from training having been magically transformed into high performers. When we talk about the engine of metrics driving change, therefore, we need to be sure that some element of coaching is highlighted as a prime activity. In this regard, three issues must be addressed:

*   Some set of coaching metrics needs to be established among the primary measurement efforts driving the initiative.

*   Managers should be required to participate in any training and be versed in the new techniques, tools, skills, and so on.

*   Managers need to be given guidance or training on how to properly coach their salespeople.

Over 10 years of research into what separates the world-class sales organization from those that are purely average has revealed that a prominent coaching culture is one of the few characteristics common to all high-performing sales organizations. Incorporating the three components described above into any performance improvement initiative will ensure that the coaching culture necessary for success is both present and active.

The last essential component of addressing Truth 4 is the implementation of a reinforcement plan. *Reinforcement* is the process of having salespeople revisit, practice, and internalize the skills, behaviors, tools, and processes that were introduced during training. Done correctly, reinforcement is offered in a prescriptive way that does not burden the user with unnecessary activity. That is, it should be fine-tuned to each person's and each manager's individual needs.

In summary, Truth 4 says organizations need to sustain momentum from the end of a training experience until sales results begin to show up. Coaching, metrics, and reinforcement are the three essential elements of making that happen. What follows is a recap of some of the main points that we've talked about with regard to changing organizations. Use it as a cheat sheet for preparing your organization for change.

Organizations do not change easily.	• Preparation • Definition of success • Balance of efficiency and effectiveness measures
Adults learn in context.	• Relevance • New tools and processes
Classrooms serve a unique purpose.	• Coaching • Practice and professional feedback in a safe environment
Change does not happen overnight.	• Measurement • Coaching • Reinforcement

We have reviewed what it takes to change both individual behavior and group behavior, emphasizing that accomplishing change requires far more than just gleaning an understanding from a book or putting people into a classroom situation. It really involves some fundamental identification in the organization of how we make changes take place. We do that through clarity of vision, strength of metrics, and association of reward and consequence. We do that on both individual bases and group bases. If you do it, you will escape price-driven selling.

This book has talked about the kinds of things that Huthwaite has discovered in its research on value creation. Several points are fundamental. Without real empirical research it's impossible to discover what the truth really is. Every salesperson and every sales manager on earth thinks he or she has the right answer. Our 30 years of research has proven that he or she seldom does. The market is always ahead of the sellers because the market is what pushes the envelope these days. And never has the market been more out of tune with the way sellers sell than it is right now. The definitions of "value" are distinctly different from what most sellers believe.

CASE STUDY: BOEING MAKES A CHANGE

Toward the end of 2003, Boeing Commercial Aviation Services (CAS) group was ready for a change. The CAS sales force was Byzantine. It was made up of five separate business units. The problem was that they all called on the same set of customers—the airlines. And you can imagine the chaos this created for account executives that represented the airplane and controlled the airline accounts. People were tripping over each other and sometimes actually competing with one another. It was not an ideal world.

Change was needed, and badly. Steve Aliment, vice president of sales for CAS, had read *SPIN® Selling*, and he was sold on the diagnostic approach to sales. He contacted Huthwaite and prepared Boeing for the change that was to follow. The CAS began by collapsing the five separate sales teams into one. They diagnosed the skills of each of their sales reps and compared the results to excellence defined by Huthwaite's research. Feature selling, which had been the staple of the five sales forces, would no longer serve. The new sales force had to be generalists rather than specialists. One-third of the sales force made the cut.

Then came the hard work. Boeing's CAS group realized that sales performance improvement would require far more than just training. Training was a vital piece of the puzzle in that it helped get everyone speaking a common language and working toward a proven methodology. They even got the marketing department oriented to the same set of principles to ensure they spoke the same language. It was part of their model. A powerful factor in the culture change took place once the sales and marketing functions spoke the same language and focused on client need. The sales generalists were now supported by product specialists each oriented to client outcome.

But success, it was determined, could be achieved only through reinforcement; the new skills must be *practiced, coached, and measured*. It was common knowledge that after most people go through training, they throw their three-ring binder from the course in a drawer and say, "That was fun." And within two months they're behaving as if they never had the training at all. To combat the usual malaise, Boeing set up an intensive program for *coaching, follow-up, and skill assessment,* ruthlessly rewarding those who performed to the new standards, and starving those who didn't. Salespeople tend to be unenthusiastic about discipline in such matters as call planning, so Boeing laid down a firm cadence of call planning, call planning review, and call planning coaching. The vice president of sales personally reviewed call plans with his salespeople before approving travel, for instance. And it went on for nearly a year until the new skills had become habit for the sales force.

Interestingly enough, in the midst of this extraordinary change initiative, Boeing's revenue goal for the CAS was not adjusted. With the sales force cut by two-thirds, the CAS nevertheless met and surpassed its sales goal for three years running. The change initiative has been a rousing and continuous success. Boeing's CAS sales force has made the transition to using a truly strategic approach, and it has enabled them to achieve their goals.

Changing either your individual behavior or the behavior of your organization to conform to what those things are takes an understanding of the content that matters and a clarity about your own situation. Huthwaite's business is helping you provide both those processes and those skills as well as that detail.

KEY POINTS

☞ Everyone wants progress, but nobody wants change. Change is not an option.

☞ Changing behavior can't be accomplished by just reading a book. Even a good book.

☞ Huthwaite has spent considerable time looking at two areas of human performance research: (a) the principles of adult learning and (b) the latest research into effective change management. An interesting conclusion has emerged from the juxtaposition of these two bodies of research.

☞ There are four truths of performance change that affect both the individual and the organization.

☞ *The Individual.* The four truths of performance change:
1. *Truth 1.* People do not change easily for these reasons: the law of first knowledge prevents easy adaptation; change requires hard work; and people usually assume that the way they are doing something is the best way to do it.
2. *Truth 2.* Adults learn in context. A generally accepted principle of adult learning is this: Adults are relevancy oriented. They need to be able to contextualize a new subject within their own framework in order to internalize it.
3. *Truth 3.* Progress requires practice (and feedback). When attempting to change a behavior, or inculcate a new one, there is no substitute for practice, repetition, and reinforcement.
4. *Truth 4.* Changes does not happen overnight. Permanent behavior change requires some form of metrics so that you can empirically judge how well you are doing.

☞ *The Organization.* The four truths of performance change:
1. *Truth 1.* Organizations don't make changes easily, nor do they make changes on demand. Only those things that are measured will get done; the engine of change is measurement.
2. *Truth 2.* Adults learn in the context of what they judge to be important and relevant to them as individuals. Just because it's good for the company does not mean it will necessarily be embraced by individual salespeople.

3. *Truth 3.* Classrooms serve a unique purpose. Classroom time should be devoted to the kinds of learning that require interpersonal practice and feedback.
4. *Truth 4.* Organizations don't make changes suddenly. Success will come only from an initiative that nests training experience in a process that includes reinforcement, coaching, and quantified, objective, individualized feedback.

TURN CONCEPT TO REALITY

In-depth research, case studies, and diagnostics
www.huthwaite.com/escaping

INDEX

About the Authors

Tom Snyder is Huthwaite, Inc.'s, senior vice president of strategy and business development. Tom advises thousands of sales decision-makers each year on topics such as consultative selling in major sales organizations, creating client value, and implementing innovative ways to strengthen competitive differentiation in an increasingly crowded marketplace. Tom is a sought-after speaker and was recently named one of the Top 100 Most Influential Sales Leaders.

Kevin Kearns is the chief executive officer of Huthwaite, Inc. He has reinvented Huthwaite to focus on driving results for clients while at the same time achieving record growth for the company. Kevin frequently advises executives at Fortune 500 companies, conducts discussions on pressing business issues with company leadership teams, and is frequently quoted in prominent business journals throughout the world.